Uniform System of Accounts and Expense Dictionary
for
Small Hotels and Motels
Revised Edition

As approved by the American Hotel & Motel Association

the EDUCATIONAL INSTITUTE
OF THE AMERICAN HOTEL & MOTEL ASSOCIATION

© 1981 by
The Educational Institute
of the American Hotel & Motel Association
1407 South Harrison Road
East Lansing, Michigan 48823

Previous edition, © 1962 by the
American Hotel & Motel Association

Printed in the United States of America

ISBN 0-86612-001-7

9/1/81

To
Joey
my ass
I don't know
what I would do
without you.

Love forever
Martha

Preface

The available data indicates there are approximately 60,000 small hotels and motels in operation in the United States. In view of the size of this phase of the accommodations industry, it was felt that a uniform system of accounts should be developed with the advantages of a standard classification of accounts. A uniform system of accounts provides a common accounting language for the industry so that when reference is made to a particular account, all concerned will understand exactly what is meant. By having the accounts of small hotels and motels classified in the same manner, industry comparisons can be made which can be helpful to management in the operations of a particular property. These comparisons will indicate whether the particular property shows up favorably or otherwise and the various facets of the operation which require attention.

In 1961, the American Hotel & Motel Association appointed the National Association of Hotel Accountants to develop a uniform system of accounts for small hotels and motels. In 1979, the Committee on Financial Management of the American Hotel & Motel Association revised the original uniform system of accounts for small hotels and motels to reflect the changes in terminology used in the accommodations industry. Raymond S. Schmidgall, CPA, instructor at Michigan State University's School of Hotel, Restaurant, and Institutional Management, worked with the following members of the committee assigned this project:

Joseph F. Cotter, Chairman, The Sheraton Corporation, Boston, Massachusetts

Walter A. (Tony) Farris, Metro Inns, Inc., Dallas, Texas

Randall L. Frazier, Marriott Hotels, Washington, D.C.

A. Neal Geller, Statler Hall, Ithaca, New York

John V. Giovenco, Hilton Hotels Corporation, Beverly Hills, California

Robert C. Jenks, Western International Hotels, Seattle, Washington

C. Everett Johnson, Pannell Kerr Forster, New York, New York

John D. Lesure, Laventhol & Horwath, Altamonte Springs, Florida

Ralph Norquist, Alameda Plaza Hotel, Kansas City, Kansas

Roy E. Posner, Loews Corporation, New York, New York

Cornelius E. Smyth, Caesars Palace, Las Vegas, Nevada

Howard White, Arthur Andersen & Co., Los Angeles, California

Introduction

There are many types of small hotels and motels. Some have restaurant facilities, others do not. Some are of a resort type with certain recreational facilities, while others are located in town and operate very similarly to hotels. This manual has been prepared to provide a basic chart of accounts for all types and sizes of operations. Due to variations in the activities between different properties, each property will use those accounts which apply to it and eliminate those which are not required. Those properties with income-producing departments for which no provision has been made in this manual should set up appropriate departmental schedules with account classifications in the same general form used in this manual. There also will be situations where a particular property may have items of income or expense of a nature not provided for in this manual, in which case the required accounts should be included in the proper departmental schedules.

The basic financial statements of any business consist of:

1. A statement of financial condition as of a certain date which sets forth the assets, liabilities and equity of the owners of the business. This statement is generally known as a Balance Sheet.

2. A statement of operations which sets forth the revenue, costs and expenses and net operating result for a given period. This statement is known by many titles, such as Statement of Profit and Loss, Statement of Income, Statement of Operations, Statement of Revenue and Expenses. In this manual we have chosen the title, Statement of Income.

3. A statement which shows the financial activities of the company between balance sheet dates. This statement is known as a Statement of Changes in Financial Position.

Section I contains an illustrative balance sheet form for a small hotel or motel. It shows the various assets and liability captions and a form of presentation in accordance with good business practice. This form of balance sheet is intended to apply to all motel/hotel properties and is to be modified by addition or deletion of captions as necessary in a particular case. The statement is followed by explanatory comments in regard to the various asset and liability categories shown on the balance sheet.

Sections II and III contain two illustrative forms of operating statements (Statement of Income) for small hotels and motels:

Section II — for those properties with operations which consist almost exclusively of rental of guest rooms and very little, if any, restaurant or other activity (including motels in which the restaurant is operated by someone else).

Section III — for properties that in addition to guest roms have food and beverage operations and other facilities.

The aforementioned groupings have been made so that those small hotels and motels which are solely or almost entirely engaged in the rental of guest rooms will have a very simplified chart of accounts and financial statements.

The accounts described in Section III are those necessary for properties with an active food and beverage operation and other facilities. Revenue and expense accounts required in order to present the financial data in the form most helpful to management are included.

Section IV contains an illustrative form of the Statement of Changes in Financial Position. Explanatory comments are included along with a brief discussion of Notes to the Financial Statements. The notes are used to describe accounting policies and procedures followed by the company and significant conditions presented in the financial statements.

Section V of this manual consists of a brief discussion of other relevant accounting/financial-oriented topics as follows:

1. Budgeting and Forecasting
2. Uniform Account Numbering System
3. Ratio Analysis

Contents

SECTION I

Balance Sheet

The balance sheet presents the assets, liabilities and equity position in a business at a stated date.

The balance sheet of a small hotel or motel may be stated much the same as that of any other business. The accounts shown in the following balance sheet will not necessarily apply in their entirety to each operation; also, some operations will have accounts which have not been provided for. Accordingly, the accounts as shown on the following balance sheet may have to be modified to meet the individual requirements, consistent with generally accepted accounting principles. In each instance, the grouping of accounts must be left to the discretion of the person preparing the statement. However, items of sufficient importance should always be shown separately.

Exhibit A

BALANCE SHEET
Assets

	Date	
	19____	19____
CURRENT ASSETS	$	$
Cash		
House Banks		
Demand Deposits		
Time Deposits and Certificates of deposit		
Marketable Securities		
Receivables		
Accounts Receivable — Trade		
Notes Receivable		
Other		
Total Receivables		
Less Allowance for Doubtful accounts		
Inventories		
Prepaid Expenses		
Other Current Assets		
Total Current Assets		
INVESTMENTS AND ADVANCES		
Affiliates		
Others		
PROPERTY AND EQUIPMENT, at cost		
Land		
Buildings		
Leasehold and Leasehold Improvements		
Construction in Progress		
Furniture and Equipment		
Less Accumulated Depreciation and Amortization		
China, Glassware, Silver, Linen, and Uniforms		
OTHER ASSETS		
Security Deposits		
Cash Surrender Value of Life Insurance, Net		
Deferred Expenses		
Preopening Expenses		
Other		
TOTAL ASSETS	$	$

See accompanying notes to financial statements.

Exhibit A *(continued)*

BALANCE SHEET
Liabilities and Shareholders' Equity

	Date	
	19	19

CURRENT LIABILITIES
Notes Payable $ $
Accounts Payable
Current Maturities on Long-term Debt
Unearned Income
Federal and State Income Taxes
Accrued Liabilities
  Salaries and Wages
  Interest
  Taxes — Other than Income
Other Current Liabilities

    Total Current Liabilities

LONG-TERM DEBT, LESS CURRENT PORTION

OTHER NON-CURRENT LIABILITIES

DEFERRED INCOME TAXES

*SHAREHOLDERS' EQUITY
Preferred Stock, Par Value $ _____
  Authorized _____ Shares
  Issued _____ Shares
Common Stock, Par Value $ _____
  Authorized _____ Shares
  Issued _____ Shares
Additional Paid-in Capital
Retained Earnings

Less Common Stock in Treasury, at cost
_____ Shares 19   ; _____ Shares 19

    Total Shareholders' Equity

COMMITMENTS AND CONTINGENCIES

TOTAL LIABILITIES AND SHAREHOLDERS' EQUITY $ $

* If Partnership or Proprietorship:
Partners' Equity (or Owners' Equity if Individual)
    A
    B

      Total Partners' Equity

ASSETS

Cash

This account includes cash on hand and demand deposits not restricted for the payment of non-current liabilities and time deposits and certificates of deposit held as short-term investments that are intended to be converted into cash in the current operating cycle.

Marketable Securities

Securities held as short-term investments that are intended to be converted into cash in the current operating cycle should be included here. The basis for valuation of such securities should be disclosed. Investments in securities of affiliated or associated companies should be shown under the caption "Investments and Advances."

Receivables

A suppporting schedule to the balance sheet may be given, subdividing the total amount of accounts receivable to suit individual requirements.

Accounts Receivable — Trade

This account should consist of the total amount due to the small hotel/motel on the open accounts carried on the guest, city, and rent ledgers. Accounts receivable due from officers and employees, unless they are minor in amount, should be shown separately. If such amounts are not expected to be collected currently they should not be included here, but should be listed separately below current assets. Accounts receivable due from affiliated companies should not be included here, but should be shown under investments and advances, below current assets.

Notes Receivable

This account should include notes receivable, which are expected to be collected within a current operating cycle. Notes receivable from officers and employees should be shown separately. Such notes which are not expected to be collected within a current operating cycle should not be included here, but should be shown under investments and advances.

Notes due from affiliated companies should not be included here, but should be shown under investments and advances, below current assets.

Allowance for Doubtful Accounts

An allowance should be provided for the portion of accounts and notes receivable estimated to be uncollectible. Such provision should be based on historical experience, specific appraisal of individual accounts or other accepted methods. Accounts which become uncollectible should be charged to this account and recoveries of accounts previously written off should be credited to it.

Inventories

The cost of merchandise held for sale and the *reserve stocks of operating supplies* which are on hand as of the balance sheet date should be included under this caption.

Prepaid Expenses

Prepaid expenses are defined as expenditures, often recurring, for benefits yet to be received within the current operating cycle. Normally the items are charged to operations on the basis of measurable benefits. Each item of prepaid expense, if material, should be listed separately either on the face of the balance sheet or in a supporting schedule. Examples are:

Insurance   Interest
Property taxes   Maintenance and service contracts
Rent   Other similar items

Other Current Assets

Other items that are reasonably expected to be realized in cash or consumed in the normal operating cycle of the business should either be separately listed or grouped under this caption.

Investments and Advances

Investments in affiliated or associated companies, and amounts due from them that are not collectible currently, should be shown here along with other securities purchased for long-term investment. The basis of valuation should be indicated.

Property and Equipment

This class of assets includes the land, building, permanent installations, furniture, fixtures, carpets, rugs, draperies, mechanical and electrical equipment, china, glassware, silver, linen and uniforms. Furniture and equipment may be subdivided to suit individual requirements.

OTHER ASSETS

Security Deposits

This account should be charged with funds deposited with telephone, water, electricity, gas, steam or similar public utility corporations and other similar type deposits.

Cash Surrender Value of Life Insurance, Net

This account should represent the accrued cash surrender value as shown by the policy, net of any loans against the policy.

Deferred Expenses

Charges for services that have been received but which are expected to benefit future periods are classified as deferred charges or deferred expenses. Examples are:

Advertising
Preopening expenses
Maintenance
Other

Deferred financing costs relating to the issuance of bonds, mortgages, or other forms of debt are also classified as deferred expenses. These costs, which are customarily amortized over the life of the issue, include items such as fees for accounting, underwriting, and legal services; printing costs; advertising expenses; and registration fees. Any unamortized discount on the issue, however, should be reported in the balance sheet as a direct deduction from the debt.

Other

Other items that cannot be included under specific groupings should be shown under this caption. Their nature, if material, should be clearly indicated on the face of the balance sheet or in a supporting schedule.

LIABILITIES AND SHAREHOLDERS' EQUITY

Notes Payable

This account should include short-term notes, separated on the balance sheet into those due to banks and those due to other creditors.

Accounts Payable

Amounts due creditors from whom provisions, stores, equipment or other purchases are made should be included in this account. Amounts due concessionaires representing collections from guests may be included with accounts payable or grouped under a separate listing.

Current Maturities on Long-Term Debt

The amounts to be retired, or sinking fund provisions to be met, within the succeeding twelve months should be stated.

Unearned Income

Under this caption should be shown the unearned portion of rentals received or charged to guests' and tenants' accounts receivable.

Federal and State Income Taxes

The amount of federal and state income taxes due for completed fiscal periods should be included here. Where provision is made for taxes payable on income subject to collection which is included in the financial statements but not in the tax returns, such as installment sales, that portion may be shown separately, if material in amount.

Accrued Liabilities

Each accrued expense item, if material in amount, should be listed separately on the balance sheet. Some of the items of expense for which it is frequently necessary to provide accruals are: salaries and wages, vacation pay, interest, steam and electricity, telephone service, water and gas.

Other Current Liabilities

Credit balances in accounts receivable and advance deposits for reservations should be shown separately under this caption, unless immaterial in amount. In addition, unclaimed wages, deposits of employees for keys, badges, lockers, and any other current liabilities not provided for above, should be included under this caption.

Long-Term Debt

Each bond issue, mortgage, or other long-term debt should be stated separately and described appropriately including the interest rate and maturity date. Any portion due within one year should be deducted and shown as current maturities on long-term debt. The unamortized discount related to long-term debt should be shown as a reduction of the total. Any defaults in sinking fund or amortization provisions should be stated.

Other Non-Current Liabilities

Includes items not listed separately above, such as deposits by tenants in accordance with the provision of long-term leases which are not returnable within the current operating cycle and deferred compensation.

Deferred Income Taxes

Deferred income taxes represent the tax effects of items reported in different periods for financial and income tax reporting purposes. The most significant of these timing differences relates to the use of accelerated depreciation for tax purposes and straight-line depreciation for financial statement purposes. Other timing differences include those arising from interest capitalized, preopening costs, and self-insured losses.

SHAREHOLDERS' EQUITY

Capital Stock

Common and preferred stock should be shown separately by classes, as described on the illustrated balance sheet.

Additional Paid-In Capital

This account includes the total amount of cash, property and other capital contributed to a corporation by its stockholders in excess of the stated and/or par value of capital stock.

Retained Earnings

The net income from operations not distributed as dividends but retained in the business is carried in this amount. Changes during the period should be shown in the financial statements.

Partners' Equity (or Owners' Equity)

If the business is carried on by a partnership or an individual, the proper title for the capital invested is "Equity." Each partner's account should be shown separately. Amounts due from partners should not be included with accounts receivable but should be deducted from their respective capital accounts. Conversely, amounts due partners should be added to their capital accounts in order to correctly show their respective interests. The same principle applies to an individual owning the business; all monies invested should be shown in one account, namely, net worth.

Commitments and Contingencies

The amount of such items should not be shown in the balance sheet but adequate disclosure should be made in the notes to the financial statements.

SECTION II

Statement of Income and Account Classifications for Small Hotels and Motels without Restaurants or with Minor Restaurant Operations (including Motels with Restaurant Leased Out)

This section of the manual presents the Statement of Income and account classifications for motels and small hotels which either do not have a restaurant or have leased out the restaurant operation. It is also intended to include those motels and small hotels which have a very limited food operation such as a continental breakfast, a low volume sandwich operation, or any other food operation which is of a minor nature.

Most properties with an operation of small to medium size without restaurant activity will find that the Balance Sheet (Section I), the Statement of Income, and the Statement of Changes in Financial Position (Section IV) will give the necessary information without any further schedules. However, it is suggested that supporting schedules be prepared in those instances where the conditions warrant. It is also suggested that statistical data in regard to room occupancy and average rate per occupied room be compiled.

In the following Statement of Income the various revenue sources are classified and shown in the first section of the statement. From "total revenue" are deducted "operating expenses" and the excess of revenue over operating expenses is captioned "total income before fixed charges."

At this point, deduction is made for items classified as fixed charges. This grouping includes the following:

Amortization
Depreciation
Fire Insurance
Interest (payable on mortgages or loans)
Personal Property Taxes
Real Estate Taxes
Rent (rent charges payable to the landlord if the land or building is leased — rental charges if furniture or equipment is rented)

The result of deducting "fixed charges" from "total income before fixed charges" is "income before income taxes" and "gain or loss on sale of property.'' From this figure, gain (loss) on the sale of property is added (subtracted) resulting in income before income taxes.

In most instances, the balance remaining after deducting income taxes represents the final operating result of the enterprise. However, there may be situations when there will be extraordinary expenses or income not applicable to regular operations. Examples of items of this nature are flood losses and fire losses. These will be shown separately after the ordinary operating result has been determined, and added to or subtracted from the ordinary operating result with proper adjustment for income taxes to determine the overall income or loss for the period.

STATEMENT OF INCOME

REVENUE $
    Rooms
    Food
    Restaurant Lease Income
    Telephone
    Gas Station — Garage — Parking
    Other Income
        Total Revenue   _____

OPERATING EXPENSES
    Payroll
    Employee Benefits
        Total Payroll and Related Expenses   _____
    Rooms
      China, Glassware and Linen
      Commissions
      Contract Cleaning
      Laundry and Dry Cleaning
      Operating Supplies
      Miscellaneous
      Reservation Expense
      Uniforms
        Total Rooms Expense   _____
    Cost of Food and Other Items Purchased for Resale
      Cost of Food Purchased and Incidental Expenses
      Cost of Gas, Oil, Auto Supplies Purchased
      Cost of Other Merchandise Purchased for Resale
        Total Cost of Food and Other Items Purchased for Resale   _____
    Property Operation, Maintenance, and Energy Costs
      Electricity
      Fuel
      Operating Supplies and Miscellaneous
      Repairs and Maintenance
      Water
        Total Property Operation, Maintenance, and Energy Costs   _____
    Swimming Pool Expense   _____
    General Expenses
      Franchise Fee
      Insurance — General
      Marketing
      Miscellaneous
      Printing, Stationery, and Postage
      Professional Fees
      Security
      Telephone and Telegrams
      Trade Association Dues and Trade Publications
      Traveling Expense
        Total General Expenses   _____
        Total Operating Expenses   _____
        Total Income Before Fixed Charges   _____

DEDUCT FIXED CHARGES   _____

INCOME BEFORE INCOME TAXES AND GAIN OR LOSS ON SALE OF PROPERTY
    Gain or Loss on Sale of Property   _____

INCOME BEFORE INCOME TAXES
    Income Taxes   _____

NET INCOME $ _____

See accompanying notes to the financial statement.

Explanation of Account Classifications for Statement of Income

In the following paragraphs are instructions as to the items which should be classified under the respective account titles shown on the Statement of Income on page 11.

REVENUE ACCOUNTS

Rooms

Rooms revenue consists of rentals for rooms and apartments, rented or leased for part-day occupancy, a full day, week, month or longer. Charges for maid or linen service should also be included.

Food

Revenue from sale of food and non-alcoholic beverages should be included under this caption.

Restaurant Lease Income

This account should be credited with rentals received from a tenant for restaurant facilities.

Telephone

Revenue received from guests for the use of telephone facilities should be credited to this account. Commissions received from the telephone company and commissions earned at pay stations and coin boxes should also be credited to this account.

Gas Station — Garage — Parking

Sales of gas, oil, and auto supplies as well as storage and parking income are to be included in this account. If the gas station — garage — parking lot is leased out, the rental should be included under this caption.

Other Income

Sundry income from miscellaneous sources should be included under this caption. It would include income from vending machines, income from merchandise sales such as postcards, souvenirs, newspapers and periodicals, commissions on guest laundry, and valet. A supporting schedule may be prepared listing the individual items comprising the total if this information is desired. Further, if any source of income is of a dollar volume that warrants presentation of the details, it should be submitted.

OPERATING EXPENSES

Payroll

All amounts of gross salaries and wages should be charged to this classification. It will include overtime pay, holiday pay, vacation pay, and all other amounts paid to employees as salaries and wages. A schedule listing the various positions (or employees) and the payroll cost of each category comprising the total payroll expense may be prepared if desired.

Employee Benefits

This classification includes those costs incurred for payroll taxes such as federal and state unemployment taxes, social security taxes, insurance applicable to employees, workmen's compensation, trades union insurance, non-union insurance, and group insurance. It would also include any expenses for social and sports activities for employees and all other costs incurred for the benefit of the employees. In many instances, management has found it helpful to have a supporting schedule setting forth the individual items comprising the total.

Rooms Expenses

China, Glassware, and Linen

Purchases of china, glassware, and linen and amounts paid for linen rental should be charged to this account.

Items included in this group are:

Ashtrays	Glasses	Shower curtains
Bath mats	Mattress protectors	Spreads
Blankets	Pillow cases	Towels
Dresser tops	Sheets	

Commissions

To this account should be charged the remuneration paid to authorized agents for room business secured for the motel, including travel agents' commissions.

14

Contract Cleaning

The cost of cleaning public space, washing windows, and exterminating done on contract by an outside firm should be included in this account.

Laundry and Dry Cleaning

The cost of laundry chargeable to the rooms operation should be charged to this account.

Operating Supplies

To this account should be charged the cost of guest supplies, cleaning supplies, and expenses applicable to the rooms operation, such as:

Guest Supplies

Bathing caps
Blotters
Bottle openers (loose)
Bridge scores, place cards and prizes
Brushes
Buttons
Candy
Coffee (free)
Combs
Corkscrews
Face cloths
Facial tissues and holders
Flowers
Fruit
Garment bags
Gifts to guests
Guest soap
Guest stationery
Hair nets
Hairpins
Hangers
Ink
Inkwells
Magazines
Matches
Needles and thread
Newspapers
Night apparel
Pens
Pins
Playing cards
Poker chips
Postcards
Shoe cloths
Talcum powder
Toilet requisites
Wash cloths
Writing supplies (guest rooms and writing rooms)

Cleaning Supplies

Acids
Alcohol
Ammonia
Ammonia water
Brass polish
Brooms
Brushes
Carpet sweepers
Carpet washer accessories
Chamois
Cheesecloths
Cleaning fluids
Contract cleaning
Deodorants
Detergents
Disinfectants
Dust cloths
Dusters
Dustpans
Exterminating
Floor polish
Floor soaps
Floor wax

(continued)

Cleaning supplies (continued)

Fly paper	Mop handles and	Soap powders
Fly swatters	wringers	Soda
Forms	Mops	Steel wool
Fumigators	Mouse traps	Vacuum cleaner
Furniture polish	Pails	accessories
Gasoline	Paint cleaners	Wall washers
Insecticides	Rags	Washing soaps and
Lemon oil	Sand	powders
Lye	Sand soap	Window cleaners'
Metal polish	Soap for cleaning	belts and equipment

Miscellaneous

In this classification should be grouped items that are not distributable under other captions, such as:

Books for guest library	Kitchenette expense
Bulletin board supplies	Licenses and permits
Candles	Postage due for guests' mail
Decorations	Safe-deposit box keys
Directories	Timetables
Firewood for lobby and rooms	Wrapping paper and twine

Reservation Expense

The cost of reservation services including telephone, teletype, and other communication expenses should be included here.

Uniforms

The cost of uniforms for employees of the rooms operation should be charged to this account; also, the cost of repairing and cleaning uniforms, the cost of buttons, braid, badges, etc., including the following:

Aprons	Dresses	Shoes
Blouses	Gloves	Smocks
Boots	Greatcoats	Suits
Caps	Jumpers	Ties
Coats	Overalls	Trousers
Collars	Raincoats	Umbrellas

Cost of Food and Other Items Purchased for Resale

Cost of Food Purchased and Incidental Expenses

This account would include amounts paid for food and non-alcoholic beverages. It would also include expenses for operating supplies and any other incidental expenses applicable to the food operation.

Cost of Gas, Oil, Auto Supplies Purchased

Purchases of gas, oil, and other items handled in connection with a gas station or garage operation should be charged to this account.

Cost of Other Merchandise Purchased for Resale

Cost of postcards, souvenirs, periodicals, and other items purchased for resale would be charged to this account.

Property Operation, Maintenance, and Energy Costs

Electricity

The cost of light and power purchased from outside producers should be charged to this account.

Fuel

This account would be charged with the cost of coal, oil, gas, or other fuel purchased.

Operating Supplies and Miscellaneous

Purchases of electric bulbs, greases, solvents, refrigeration supplies, fuses, charges for removal of waste, and sundry other items would be included under this category.

Repairs and Maintenance

This expense classification should be charged with all costs in connection with the repair and maintenance of the building, equipment, furniture and fixtures, and other expenditures necessary to keep the property in operating condition. All repair and maintenance charges are included in this category. Expenses of the following nature should be included:

Building repairs
Electrical and mechanical equipment
Furniture and equipment repairs

(continued)

Repairs and maintenance (continued)

Maintenance of grounds
Painting and decorating
Plumbing, heating, air conditioning repairs
Swimming pool repairs

If the amounts expended for repairs and maintenance are substantial, it would be desirable to prepare a schedule listing the various items included.

Water

This account would be charged with cost of water purchased and the costs for water purification and water tests.

Swimming Pool Expense

Expenses incurred in the operation of the swimming pool would be charged to this account. These items would include supplies such as chemicals for water treatment, cleaning supplies, and other incidental supplies. Repair expenses should be charged to repairs and maintenance.

General Expenses

Franchise Fee

This account should be charged with amounts paid as franchise fees.

Insurance – General

All insurance premiums (exclusive of fire insurance on buildings and contents) should be charged to this account, including the following:

Boiler liability	Forgery	Products liability
Burglary	Fraud	Property damage
Elevator liability	Holdup	Public liability
Fidelity bonds	Life insurance	Robbery
Flywheel liability	Lost and damaged goods	Use and occupancy

Marketing

All costs incurred for publicity and promotion of the property should be charged to this classification. Ads in newspapers, periodicals, journals, and costs incidental thereto for preparation of copy would be included in this category. Costs of contributions to local convention bureau activities, radio and television broadcasting, entertainment, travel, printing and stationery and brochures would also be charged to this classification.

Miscellaneous

Under this classification should be grouped items which are not distributable under other captions, including the following:

Axes — fire
Carfares
Cash overages and shortages
Chemicals for fire extinguishers
Christmas expense
Commissions on credit card
    charges
Contributions and donations,
    other than promotional
Credit and collection expenses
Employee investigation
Exchange on bank checks and
    currency
Executive office expenses
Express charges, not provided
    for elsewhere
Fire bucket sand
Freight charges, not provided
    for elsewhere
Help wanted ads
Housing and lodging of employees

Internal communicating system
Licenses, not applicable to any
    particular department
Loss and damage to guest property
Mail bags
Mail chute rental
Management fees
Paper towels for employees
Protective service cost
Safe-deposit box rental
Stock transfer agents fees,
    transfer fees
Storage of equipment
Street cleaning and sprinkling
Taxicab fares
Ticker service
Trucking, not provided for
    elsewhere
Uncollectible accounts
Uniforms
Western Union time service

Printing, Stationery, and Postage

The cost of printed forms, service manuals, stationery, and office supplies should be charged to this account as well as all postage charges.

The following list indicates the nature of the items to be included in this account:

Adding machine
    paper
Bank checks
Billing machine
    supplies
Binders
Blotters
Books of account

Books — record
Carbon paper
Clips
Envelopes
Fountain pens
Guest ledgers
Ink
Ink pads

Ink wells
Mucilage
Office supplies
Paper clips
Paste
Pen holders

(continued)

Printing, stationery & postage (continued)

Pen points	Report covers	Staples
Pencils	Rubber bands	Stationery
Pens	Rubber stamps	Transcripts
Pins	Stamp pads	Typewriter ribbons

Professional Fees

Charges by public accountants and lawyers should be charged to this account.

Security

The cost of providing security for guests, personnel, and property should be charged to this account, including alarm, armored car, and guard services.

Telephone and Telegrams

Bills received for telephone and telegraph charges should be entered in this account. Any charges for rental of equipment, transfer charges, etc., should also be included in this account.

Trade Association Dues and Trade Publications

The cost of representation of the property in business organizations and subscriptions to papers, magazines and books for the use of the executives and employees should be charged to this account.

Traveling Expenses

The cost of travel for business purposes should be charged to this account; however, traveling in connection with business promotion should be charged to marketing.

Fixed Charges

Fixed charges include rent, real estate taxes, personal property taxes, fire insurance, interest expense, depreciation, and amortization.

Gain or Loss on Sale of Property

The gain or loss on sale of property is determined by subtracting the net book value (cost less accumulated depreciation) from the proceeds received from the sale of the property. If the proceeds exceed the net book value, the result is a gain, while the reverse results in a loss.

Income Taxes

Income taxes include federal, state, and local income taxes.

Simplified Bookkeeping for Small Hotels and Motels Without Restaurants

The foregoing pages contained a simplified set of accounts and statements for small hotels and motels which either do not have a restaurant operation or have a very limited food operation. Properties that operate in this manner and adopt the simplified system of accounts may also operate with a simplified system of bookkeeping which will provide the necessary information for the financial statements.

Every business enterprise must keep a record of cash received and cash paid out. Accordingly, the simplest system of bookkeeping would be limited to record keeping on a cash basis. Owners and/or operators who wish to keep their records on this basis will find that if the cash transactions are entered on cash sheets following the forms shown on page 23, the bookkeeping and preparation of financial statements will be greatly facilitated.

On page 23, there is a suggested form of Cash Receipts record. All cash receipts should be entered on the Cash Receipts record and deposited intact in the bank. If it is necessary to make minor cash disbursements in cash (other than by check) the payments should be made from a petty cash fund. It is suggested that this fund be on an imprest basis — a fund for a fixed amount which would be reimbursed from time to time from the general bank account.

The cash received from each guest would be analyzed as to the items covered. Some collections might cover cash received for other than rooms and these items should be entered in the appropriate columns.

At the close of the month the totals of the various columns shown on the Cash Receipts record should be posted to the proper accounts in the ledger. In the case of the items shown in columns 7 and 8 GENERAL, the individual items should be posted to the respective ledger accounts shown in column 7.

Cash disbursements should be entered in the Cash Disbursements record with the check number and amount of the check entered in columns 1 and 2. Entry of the distribution to the account classification should be made in columns 3 to 13 inclusive to the extent applicable. In cases of amounts chargeable to Rooms, to Cost of Items Purchased for Resale, to Property Operation, Maintenance and Energy Costs, to General Expenses, or to Sundry, the name of the appropriate account classification should be inserted along with the proper amount.

Swimming pool expenses should be entered in columns 13 and 14. The Swimming Pool account classification should be shown in column 13 and the amount of expense shown in column 14 and subsequently posted to the Swimming Pool account in the ledger.

A petty cash disbursement record in the same form as the Cash Disbursements record (except for check number which should be eliminated) should be used for petty cash disbursements. At the time the reimbursement check is drawn on the general bank account, the disbursement should show on that account and distribution of the charges should be made to the respective account classifications to which they apply as shown by the petty cash record.

At the end of the month the money columns of the Cash Disbursement record should be footed and the total of columns 3 through 14 should agree with the total of column 2. Postings to the ledger should be made from the totals for columns 2, 3, and 4. The items entered in columns 5 and 6, Account and Amount, should be posted individually to the respective accounts to which they apply. This same procedure should be followed for columns 7-8, 9-10, 11-12 and 13-14.

The forms will give a complete record of all cash transactions of the business, and the accounts as shown on the ledger will reflect the financial condition and the operation of the enterprise on a cash basis. However, if there are amounts due to the small hotel or motel or amounts payable for supplies or services which have not been paid, they would not be reflected on the records. Where the amounts due and the amounts unpaid are minor, it is sometimes considered practicable not to do the necessary bookkeeping to record these items. In many cases in order to have the true financial picture, it is essential that the receivables and payables be entered on the records. This type of record keeping is known as accrual basis.

In order to present the financial statements in conformity with generally accepted accounting principles (accrual basis) the receivables and payables can be recorded in the following manner.

Amounts receivable should be listed on a separate sheet of the Cash Receipts journal and analyzed by type of charge to the proper classifications. The entries to the ledger are made exactly in the same manner as from the Cash Receipts sheet except that instead of the heading Amount Received on column 1, the heading would be changed to Accounts Receivable and posted to that account in the ledger. At the end of the following month, the postings made from this sheet to the ledger for the month before should be *reversed* and a new sheet prepared showing amounts receivable at the end of the current month which should be posted to the ledger in the same manner as the month before.

Amounts payable should be listed on a separate sheet of the Cash Disbursements journal and analyzed by type of item to the proper classifications. The entries to the ledger should be made exactly in the same manner as from the Cash Disbursements sheet except that the total of column 2 (Amount) should be posted to Accounts Payable in the ledger. At the close of the following month, the postings made from this sheet to the ledger for the month before should be *reversed* and a new sheet prepared showing amounts payable at the end of the current month which should be posted to the ledger in the same manner as the month before.

CASH RECEIPTS

				1	1A	2
Date	Room No.	Name	Deposit	Amount Received	Sales Tax	Rooms

NOTE: 1A — This column to be used for sales taxes in those localities where required.

CASH DISBURSEMENTS

		1	2	3	4	5	6	7	8
		Check				Payroll Taxes,	Rooms		Cost of Items Purchased for Resale
Date	Paid To	No.	Amount	Payroll		etc.	Account	Amount	Account	Amount

Month of _____

3	4	5	6		7	8
Food	Telephone	Gas Station Garage Parking	Other Income		General	
			Source	Amount	Account	Amount

Month of _____

9	10	11	12	13	14	
Property Operation, Maintenance, and Energy Costs		General Expenses		Sundry		
Account	Amount	Account	Amount	Account	Amount	

SECTION III

Statement of Income for the Small Hotel and Motel Including Operation of Restaurant and Other Supplementary Departments

This section of the manual presents a Statement of Income, with subsidiary schedules and account classifications, for the larger type of small hotel or motel which operates a restaurant, bar, or other subsidiary departments. Previous comments in regard to the Balance Sheet also apply to this type of operation. However, since operations of this nature are so much more extended and varied, the Statement of Income for this type of operation has been expanded and departmentalized, and is supported by detailed subsidiary schedules.

The first grouping on the Statement of Income, Exhibit B, covers the revenue and expenses of the operated departments. Results are shown in columns for Net Revenues, Cost of Sales, Payroll and Related Expenses, Other Expenses, and Income (Loss), each line being a very brief summary of the supporting subsidiary schedule which shows the departmental operations in detail. From the income derived from the operated departments, expenses are deducted which are considered applicable to the entire property and not easily allocated to the operated departments. This group of expenses is also supported by detailed subsidiary schedules. After deducting this group of expenses, the result is Total Income Before Fixed Charges.

From Total Income Before Fixed Charges, fixed charges also supported by detailed subsidiary schedules are subtracted.

From this point, the Gain (loss) on Sale of Property is added (deducted) resulting in Income Before Income Taxes. Income Taxes are subtracted from Income Before Income Taxes resulting in Net Income. A detailed subsidiary schedule of income taxes should be provided to support income taxes expense.

Exhibit B

STATEMENT OF INCOME

	Schedule	Net Revenues	Cost of Sales	Payroll and Related Expenses	Other Expenses	Income (Loss)
OPERATED DEPARTMENTS		$	$	$	$	$
Rooms	B-1					
Food and Beverage	B-2					
Telephone	B-3					
Gift Shop	B-4					
Gas Station — Garage — Parking	B-5					
Other Operated Departments	B-					
Rentals and Other Income	B-6					
TOTAL DEPARTMENTAL REVENUE, EXPENSE, AND INCOME (LOSS)						
UNDISTRIBUTED OPERATING EXPENSES						
Administrative and General Expenses	B-7					
Marketing	B-8					
Property Operation, Maintenance & Energy Costs	B-9					
Total Undistributed Operating Expenses						
TOTAL INCOME BEFORE FIXED CHARGES		$	$	$	$	$
Rent	B-10					
Property Taxes	B-10					
Insurance	B-10					
Interest	B-10					
Depreciation and Amortization	B-10					
INCOME BEFORE INCOME TAXES AND GAIN OR LOSS ON SALE OF PROPERTY						
Gain or Loss on Sale of Property	B-10					
INCOME BEFORE INCOME TAXES						
Income Taxes	B-10					
NET INCOME					$	

ROOMS

REVENUE $

    Guest Rooms

    Transient

    Permanent

        Total Revenue

Allowances

Net Revenue

EXPENSES

    Salaries and Wages

    Employee Benefits

        Total Payroll and Related Expenses

    China, Glassware, and Linen

    Commissions

    Contract Cleaning

    Laundry and Dry Cleaning

    Operating Supplies

    Other Operating Expenses

    Reservation Expense

    Uniforms

        Total Other Expenses

DEPARTMENTAL INCOME (LOSS) $

Rooms Statistics

Rooms Occupied and Vacant

    Occupied by Guests

    Complimentary

    Vacant

    Out of Order

        Total Available Rooms

    House Use

        Net Rooms Available

Percentage of Rooms Occupied and Vacant   %

    Occupied by Guests

    Complimentary

    Vacant

    Out of Order

    House Use

Average Revenue per Guest Occupied Room per Day $

Total Number of Guest Days

Average Revenue per Guest per Day $

Rooms

REVENUE

Guest Rooms

Room revenue consists of revenue derived from rooms and apartments, rented or leased for part-day occupancy, a full day, week, month or longer. Charges for maid or linen service should also be included. Where rooms and meals are sold at an inclusive price, a division should be made of the sales between rooms and food to assure that each department receives its equitable share.

Allowances

Allowances represent rebate and overcharges of revenue (not known at the time of sale but adjusted at a subsequent date).

Net Revenues

The total of revenues less allowances will constitute the net revenues of the Rooms Department.

EXPENSES

Salaries and Wages

For the classification of employees included in this group, see Rooms Department payroll schedule, page 70.

Employee Benefits

This account is charged with vacation and holiday pay and the allocated portion of payroll taxes and social insurance and other related expenses properly applicable to this department. The cost of food and beverage furnished to employees, and other amounts such as Christmas bonus and severance pay, are also included in this account.

China, Glassware and Linen

Items included in this group are:

Ashtrays	Dresser trays	Shower curtains
Bath mats	Glasses	Spreads
Blankets	Mattress protectors	Towels
Candlesticks	Pillow cases	Tumblers
Carafes	Sheets	Water pitchers
Dresser tops		

Amounts paid for linen rental should be charged to this account.

Commissions

To this account should be charged the remuneration paid to authorized agents for room business secured for the motel/hotel, including travel agents' commissions and commissions to rental agents for leases. In the case of leases, the charges would be prorated over the term of the lease.

Contract Cleaning

The cost of cleaning lobbies and public rooms, washing windows, exterminating, and disinfecting done on contract by outside concerns should be included in this account.

Laundry and Dry Cleaning

The cost of laundry and dry cleaning chargeable to the rooms department, as indicated by bills of outside laundries, should be charged to this account. For work done by the entity's laundry, see House Laundry Schedule B-12.

Operating Supplies

Guest Supplies

The cost of supplies furnished to guest rooms and writing desks should be charged to this account, including the following:

Bathing caps	Flowers	Newspapers
Blotters	Fruit	Night apparel
Bottle openers	Garment bags	Pens
(loose)	Gifts to guests	Pins
Bridge scores, place	Guest soap	Playing cards
cards and prizes	Guest stationery	Poker chips
Brushes	Hair nets	Shoe cloths
Buttons	Hairpins	Talcum powder
Candy	Hangers	Toilet requisites
Combs	Inks	Wash cloths
Corkscrews	Inkwells	Writing supplies
Face cloths	Magazines	(guest rooms
Facial tissues and	Matches	and writing
holders	Needles and thread	rooms)

Cleaning Supplies

To this account should be charged the cost of cleaning supplies and expenses of the Rooms Department, such as:

Acids	Dusters	Pails
Alcohol	Dustpans	Paint cleaners
Ammonia	Floor polish	Rags
Ammonia water	Floor soaps	Sand
Brass polish	Floor wax	Sand soap
Brooms	Fly paper	Soap for cleaning
Brushes	Fly swatters	Soap powders
Carpet sweepers	Fumigators	Soda
Carpet washer	Furniture polish	Steel wool
accessories	Gasoline	Vacuum cleaner
Chamois	Insecticides	accessories
Cheesecloths	Lemon oil	Wall washers
Cleaning fluids	Lye	Washing soaps
Deodorants	Metal polish	and powders
Detergents	Mop handles	Window cleaners'
Disinfectants	Mops	belts and
Dust cloths	Mouse traps	equipment

Printing and Stationery

The cost of printed forms, service manuals, stationery and office supplies should be charged to this account when used by employees of the department. Excluded from this category are guest writing materials included in guests supplies and cashiers' and bill clerks' supplies which are charged to administrative and general expenses.

The following list indicates the nature of the items to be included in this account:

Binders	Clips	Ink
Blotters	Desk pads	Ink pads
Books — record	Envelopes — safety	Inkwells
Carbon paper	Floor plans	Mucilage
Charge vouchers	Fountain pens	Paper clips

(continued)

Printing and Stationery (continued)

Paste	Rack cards	Rubber stamps
Pen holders	Reports for	Stamp pads
Pen points	housekeeper and	Staples
Pencils	maids	Typewriter ribbons
Pens	Rubber bands	Vouchers

Other Operating Expenses

Under this classification should be grouped those items that are not distributable under other captions, such as:

Books for guest library	Help wanted ads for rooms employees
Bulletin board supplies	Kitchenette expenses
Candles	Licenses and permits
Decorations	Postage due for guests' mail
Directories	Safe-deposit box keys
Employee transportation	Timetables
Firewood for lobby	Wrapping paper and twine

Reservation Expenses

The cost of reservation service, central reservation system, including telephone, telegram, and teletype expenses should be charged to this account.

Uniforms

The cost of uniforms for employees of the Rooms Department should be charged to this account; also, the cost of repairing and cleaning uniforms, the cost of buttons, braid, badges, etc., including the following:

Aprons	Dresses	Shoes
Blouses	Gloves	Smocks
Boots	Greatcoats	Suits
Caps	Jumpers	Ties
Coats	Overalls	Trousers
Collars	Raincoats	Umbrellas

Food and Beverage

Many small hotels and motels have facilities selling both food and beverage, although in some areas the service of either may predominate. It is impractical to separate accurately the costs of operation, other than direct cost of sales, because the employees generally handle both products; and other goods and services that are purchased may not be readily identifiable as either food or beverage expense. Although it is possible to make allocations of food and beverage, a determination of departmental income by sales outlet is preferable.

The statement and description that follows is intended for use as a summary of the operation of the food and beverage facilities. It should be supported by detailed schedules for each outlet, generally following the same format as the summary.

Schedule B-2

FOOD AND BEVERAGE

	Current Period
REVENUE	$
Food	
Beverage	
Total	
ALLOWANCES	
NET REVENUE	
OTHER INCOME	
Total	
COST OF SALES	
Cost of Food Consumed	
Less Cost of Employees' Meals	
Net Cost of Food Sales	
Cost of Beverage Sales	
Net Cost of Sales	
GROSS PROFIT	
EXPENSES	
Salaries and Wages	
Employee Benefits	
Total Payroll and Related Expenses	
Other Expenses	
China, Glassware, Silver and Linen	
Contract Cleaning	
Kitchen Fuel	
Laundry and Dry Cleaning	
Licenses	
Music and Entertainment	
Operating Supplies	
Other Operating Expenses	
Uniforms	
Total Other Expenses	
TOTAL EXPENSES	
DEPARTMENTAL INCOME (LOSS)	$

Food and Beverage
REVENUE

Food

This account should be credited with revenue derived from food sales. The sales may be classified by dining rooms, room service, and banquets. Sales do not include meals charged on employees' (staff) checks; the total of these, reduced to cost, should be deducted from the cost of food consumed and charged to the respective departments as employees' meals. Commissary and steward's sales should be credited to the cost of food consumed where there is no income, or where the income is merely nominal. Where the income on such sales is of sufficient importance to warrant it, the amount should be included in gross sales, and the cost of such sales charged to cost of food consumed. Sales of grease and bones will be credited to cost of food consumed, and not included in gross sales.

Where a small hotel or motel is operated on the American plan, a division should be made between sales of rooms and food, to assure that each department receives its equitable share of revenue.

Beverage

This account should be credited with revenue derived from beverage sales. The sales may be classified by dining rooms, room service, banquets and public bars; also for the purpose of further analysis, the sales may be segregated into wines, spirits and liquors, beers and ales, and mineral waters, or such other classification as may be desirable. Sales do not include beverages served on officers' checks; the total of these, reduced to cost, should be deducted from cost of beverage sales and charged to the respective departments as employees' meals or entertainment. Sales of bottles and barrels should be credited to cost of beverage sales and not be included in gross sales.

Allowances

Allowances represent rebates and overcharges of revenue (not known at the time of sale) but adjusted at a subsequent date.

Net Revenue

The total revenue, less allowances, will constitute the net revenue.

Other Income

This caption should include revenue from sources other than the sale of food and beverages. In the detailed schedules for the various outlets, sources such as the following could be listed:

Public Room Rentals

Revenue derived from the rental of public rooms should be included under this caption.

Cover and Minimum Charges

These charges represent the revenue derived from charging a specific rate per person, intended to defray such expenses as music and entertainment.

Sundry Banquet Income

Where occasional sales of goods or services are made in connection with banquets, the respective expense items such as music, decorations, and souvenirs should be credited. Where, however, the sales are of sufficient importance to make it desirable to determine the income on such sales, accounts should be opened as required, and the net income carried as sundry banquet income.

Miscellaneous

This account should include any income or revenue not otherwise provided for, such as ice service to guest rooms. If substantial in amount it should be identified by specific captions.

COST OF SALES

Food

The cost of food consumed includes all food served to both guests and employees, at gross invoice price, less trade discounts (but not cash discounts), plus transportation, storage, and delivery charges. To this cost should be credited commissary and steward's sales, including the sales of grease and bones.

The cost of employees' meals should be deducted from the cost of food consumed, the contra entry for which should be charged against the respective departments whose employees are served, as designated by the payroll schedule, page 71 of this manual. The cost of employees' meals varies to such an extent that each small hotel or motel is obliged to compute its own cost, either by an exact cost system, as in the larger hotels, or at a fixed price per meal where the determination of an exact cost would be unwarranted. Particular care should be exercised in the credit given for employees' meals, so as not to distort the net cost of sales.

Beverage

The cost of beverage sales represents the cost of wines, liquors, beers; also, mineral waters, fruits, syrups, sugar, bitters, and all other materials served as beverages or used in the preparation of mixed drinks, including those served to both guests and employees, at gross invoice price less trade discounts (but not cash discounts), plus import duties, transportation, storage, and delivery charges, and taxes determined on the basis of quantity and alcoholic content of beverage purchased or consumed.

The cost of beverage sales should be credited with deposit refunds and sales of empty bottles, barrels, and other materials previously charged as a cost to this account.

The cost of employees' beverages should be deducted from the cost of beverage sales, the contra entry for which would be a charge against the respective departments whose employees are served, as designated in the payroll schedule.

Net Cost of Sales

The net cost of sales results from the addition of the net cost of food sales and the cost of beverage sales.

EXPENSES

Salaries and Wages

For the classification of employees included in this group, see payroll schedule, page 71.

Employee Benefits

This account is charged with vacation and holiday pay and the allocated portion of payroll taxes and social insurance and other related expenses properly applicable to this department. The cost of food and beverage furnished to Food and Beverage Department employees, and other amounts such as Christmas bonus and severance pay, are also included in this account.

China, Glassware, Silver and Linen

Items included in the group as food expenses are:

Bowls	Ladles	Table cloths
Coffee pots	Napkins	Table protectors
Compotes	Pitchers	Table tops
Cups	Plates	Teapots
Doilies	Platters	Towels
Drinking glasses	Saucers	Trays
Flatware	Serving dishes	Tumblers
Goblets		

The cost of beverage glassware to be charged to this account should include all of the various types of glasses used in the serving of wines, liquors, and other beverages.

The cost of rented linen services should also be charged to this account.

Contract Cleaning

The cost of cleaning dining rooms, public rooms and pantries, washing windows in dining rooms, exterminating and disinfecting done on contract by outside concerns, should be included in this account.

Kitchen Fuel

To this account should be charged the cost of fuel used for cooking, including the following:

Charcoal	Food warmer supplies	Gas governors
Coal	Gas	Steam

Where all or the major part of cooking or baking is done by electricity the current should be metered, or otherwise accurately determined, and the cost charged to this account. Where electricity is used only incidentally, the determination of such cost is not warranted.

Laundry and Dry Cleaning

The cost of the laundry chargeable to the Food and Beverage Department, as designated by bills of outside laundries, should be charged to this account. For work done by the property's own laundry, see house laundry schedule, page 68 of the manual.

This account should also be charged with the cost of dry cleaning curtains, draperies, hangings, and lamp shades and washing or cleaning awnings, carpets and rugs, window shades, and furniture coverings in the various dining and public rooms.

Licenses

This account should be charged with all federal, state, and municipal licenses.

Music and Entertainment

This account should be charged with the cost of the following:

Films	Piano rental	Records
Mechanical music	Professional	Royalties
Music license	entertainers	Sheet music
Musicians	Programs	Tuning pianos

Operating Supplies

The items to be included in this account are described below:

Cleaning Supplies

The cost of supplies to keep the food and beverage areas of the small hotel or motel and the equipment used in the storage, preparation, and service of food and beverage in a clean and sanitary condition, including:

Brooms	Dishwashing	Polishes
Brushes	compounds	Silver cleaners
Carpet sweepers	Disinfectants	Soap powders
Cleaning compounds	Insecticides	Soaps
Detergents	Mops	Steel wool
	Pails	

Guest Supplies

Boutonnieres	Favors	Matches
Candy	Gifts	Menus
Cigars & cigarettes	Ice	Newspapers
Corsages		Souvenirs

Paper Supplies

The cost of paper supplies used by the Food and Beverage Department, including:

Cardboard boxes	Holders	Plates
Chop frills	Liners	Ramekins
Cups	Liquid containers	Souffle cups
Doilies	Napkins	Straws
Filter paper	Parchment	Tortoni cups
	Pastry bags	Waxed paper

Printing and Stationery

The cost of printed forms, office supplies, stationery and similar items used by employees of the Food and Beverage Department, including:

Adding machine tapes	Desk pads	Signature books
Announcement cards	Paper clips	Stamp pads
Binders	Pencils	Staplers
Books — records	Pens	Staples
Checking supplies	Restaurant checks	Typewriter ribbons
Clips	Rubber bands	Vouchers
	Rubber stamps	Waiters' books

Other Operating Expenses

Under this classification should be grouped such food and beverage expense items as are not distributed under other captions, including the following:

Banquet expense	Food inspection	Sawdust
Bar expense	Galax leaves	Signs
Coffee bags	Garbage cans	Twine
Commissions	Gas range rental	Utensils
Employees' transportation	Laboratory costs	Warehouse cost

Uniforms

The cost of uniforms for employees of the Food and Beverage Department should be charged to this account; also, the cost of repairing and cleaning uniforms, the cost of buttons, braids, badges, and similar items, including the following:

Aprons	Dresses	Smocks
Blouses	Gloves	Suits
Caps	Shirtfronts	Ties
Coats	Shoes	Trousers
Collars		

TELEPHONE

	Current Period $
REVENUE	
Local	
Long Distance	
Service Charges	
Commissions — Local	
Commissions — Long Distance	_____
Total	_____
COST OF CALLS	
Local	
Long Distance	_____
Total	_____
Rental of Equipment	_____
Depreciation of Telephone Equipment	_____
Total Cost of Calls	_____
GROSS PROFIT (LOSS)	_____
EXPENSES	
Salaries and Wages	
Employee Benefits	_____
Total Payroll and Related Expenses	_____
Other Expenses	
Total Expenses	_____
DEPARTMENTAL INCOME (LOSS)	$ _____

Telephone

REVENUE

This account should be credited with revenue derived from the use of telephone facilities by guests, including local calls, long distance calls, service charges, and commissions less allowances and rebates. The account should not be credited with any amounts for telephone service used by the management or other departments of the property.

COST OF CALLS

The sum total of the amounts billed by the telephone company for local calls and long distance calls constitutes the gross cost of calls. To the cost thus determined there should be added, in order to arrive at the total cost of calls, the charges made by the telephone company for switchboard and telephone equipment in guest rooms or elsewhere in the property.

Should the bills of the telephone company not be available at the time of closing the books, the gross cost should be estimated, accrued and applied to the period. Adjustments disclosed when the telephone bills are received should be made in the following month.

The cost of internal communicating systems should not be charged to this account but included in the account provided under administrative and general expenses.

DEPRECIATION OF TELEPHONE EQUIPMENT

This account should be charged with the depreciation expense applicable to purchased telephone equipment and systems.

GROSS PROFIT (LOSS)

The gross profit (loss) is the balance remaining after deducting from revenues the cost of calls.

EXPENSES

Salaries and Wages

For the classification of employees included in this group, see Telephone Department payroll schedule, page 72.

Employee Benefits

This account is charged with vacation and holiday pay and the allocated portion of payroll taxes and social insurance and other related expenses properly applicable to this department. The cost of food and beverage furnished to employees, and other amounts such as Christmas bonus and severance pay, are also included in this account.

Other Expenses

This account should include charges by the telephone company for changes in location of equipment, printing and stationery, and other operating expenses.

Schedule B-4

GIFT SHOP

	Current Period
REVENUE	$
COST OF GOODS SOLD	
GROSS PROFIT	
EXPENSES	
Salaries and Wages	
Employee Benefits	
Total Payroll and Related Expenses	
Operating Supplies	
Other Operating Expenses	
Total Expenses	
DEPARTMENTAL INCOME (LOSS)	$

Gift Shop

REVENUE

This account should be credited with revenue derived from sales of candies, confections, food products, novelties and other commodities, classified as desired.

COST OF GOODS SOLD

The cost of goods sold represents the purchase price of merchandise, commodities and products sold, less trade discounts, plus transportation and delivery charges. The amount may be determined by the value of inventory at the beginning of the period, plus total purchases, less closing inventory.

GROSS PROFIT

The gross profit is the balance after deducting from revenues the cost of goods sold.

EXPENSES

Salaries and Wages

For the classification of employees included in this group see Gift Shop payroll schedule, page 72.

Employee Benefits

This account is charged with vacation and holiday pay and the allocated portion of payroll taxes and social insurance and other related expenses properly applicable to this department. The cost of food and beverage furnished to employees, and other amounts such as Christmas bonus and severance pay, are also included in this account.

Operating Supplies

The cost of various supplies used in this department should be charged to this account. The following should be included:

Cleaning supplies	Pens and pencils	Silver cleaner
Glassware	Sales checks	Twine
Packing supplies	Scotch tape	Wrapping paper
Paper cups		

If a particular item or group of similar items are of substantial amount, a separate classification should be considered.

Other Operating Supplies

Under this classification should be grouped those items that are not distributable under other captions.

GAS STATION — GARAGE — PARKING

	Current Period
REVENUES	
Parking and Storage Income	$
Merchandise	
Other Service Income	_____
Total Revenue	_____
COST OF SALES	_____
GROSS PROFIT	_____
EXPENSES	
Salaries and Wages	
Employee Benefits	_____
Total Payroll and Related Expenses	_____
Other Expenses	
Licenses	
Management Fee	
Operating Supplies	
Other Operating Expenses	
Uniforms	_____
Total Expenses	_____
DEPARTMENTAL INCOME (LOSS)	$_____

Gas Station — Garage — Parking

REVENUE

Parking and Storage Income

This account should be credited with the fees received for parking services rendered.

Merchandise

Revenue from sales of merchandise should be credited to this account. Where a particular item sold is material in amount in relation to total revenue generated by the department, descriptive captions of each revenue should be shown.

Other Service Income

This account should include washing and polishing, repairs and miscellaneous.

COST OF SALES

The cost of goods sold represents the purchase price of merchandise sold. The amount may be determined by the value of inventory at the beginning of the period, plus total purchases, less closing inventory. Cost of sales should have the same classifications as revenue. It is essential that the items charged to the respective classifications of cost of sales be of the same classifications as the items credited to the same revenue classifications.

GROSS PROFIT

The gross profit is the balance after deducting from revenues the cost of sales.

EXPENSES

Salaries and Wages

For the classification of employees included in this group, see Gas Station — Garage — Parking payroll schedule, page 72.

Employee Benefits

This account is charged with vacation and holiday pay and the allocated portion of payroll taxes and social insurance and other related expenses properly applicable to this department. The cost of food and beverage furnished to employees, and other amounts such as Christmas bonus and severance pay, are also included in this account.

Licenses

This account should be charged with the cost of all licenses and permits that are necessary for the operation of this department.

Management Fee

This account should be charged with the fee paid to professional garage operators for the management of the small hotel or motel garage.

Operating Supplies

This account should be charged with the cost of such items as gas, oil, and parts used in the operation of the garage parking lot which are not chargeable to a customer.

Other Operating Expenses

Items which are not classified under other captions should be charged to this account. If a particular item or group of similar items are of substantial amount, a separate classification should be considered.

Uniforms

The cost of uniforms for employees of this department should be charged to this account; also, the cost of repairing and cleaning uniforms, the cost of buttons, braids, and badges.

Other Operated Departments

In the industry, the same or similar services may be operated by the small hotel or motel or operated by others under rental or concession agreements. When the small hotel or motel operates the individual department, rather than a concessionaire, a separate schedule should be prepared for each department.

Generally speaking, operated departments which would fall into these categories would include, but not be limited to, the following:

Apparel shop
Barber shop
Beauty salon
Checkrooms and washrooms
Cigar and newsstand
Liquor store
Valet

Schedule B-

OTHER OPERATED DEPARTMENTS

	Current Period $
REVENUE	
Services	
Sales of Merchandise	
Total Revenue	_____
ALLOWANCES	
NET REVENUE	
COST OF MERCHANDISE SOLD	_____
GROSS PROFIT	_____
EXPENSES	
Salaries and Wages	
Employee Benefits	
Total Payroll and Related Expenses	_____
Other Expenses	
China and Glassware	
Contract Services	
Laundry	
Linen	
Operating Supplies	
Other Operating Expenses	
Uniforms	
Total Other Expenses	_____
TOTAL EXPENSES	_____
DEPARTMENTAL INCOME (LOSS)	$ _____

REVENUE

Revenue should include all revenue derived from services and/or merchandise sold by the particular department. When a particular service or certain merchandise is a material part of the total revenue generated by the department, descriptive captions describing each source of revenue should be shown.

ALLOWANCES

Allowances represent rebates and overcharges of revenues (not known at the time of sale) but adjusted at a subsequent date.

COST OF MERCHANDISE SOLD

The cost of merchandise sold represents the purchase price of such merchandise, less trade discounts (but not cash discounts), plus freight, storage, delivery, and other charges related to placing the merchandise for sale. The amount of the cost of merchandise sold should be based upon periodic inventories taken in order to accurately reflect actual cost of merchandise sold.

Where material, the type of merchandise should be described and related to the appropriate caption of revenue.

GROSS PROFIT

The gross profit is the balance after deducting from revenues the cost of merchandise sold.

EXPENSES

Expenses include the direct payroll of salaries and wages plus related employee benefits, and such other expenses as china and glassware, contract services, laundry, linen, operating supplies, and uniforms. Any other expenses related to such departments, which are material in amount, should be described separately. Otherwise, they can be shown in a general caption entitled Other Operating Expenses.

RENTALS AND OTHER INCOME

	Current Period $
SPACE RENTALS	
Stores	
Offices	
Clubs	
Others	
Total Rentals	_____
CONCESSIONS	_____
Total Concessions	_____
COMMISSIONS	
Laundry	
Valet	
Other	
Total Commissions	_____
INTEREST INCOME	_____
VENDING MACHINES	_____
CASH DISCOUNTS EARNED	_____
SALVAGE	_____
MISCELLANEOUS	_____
TOTAL RENTALS AND OTHER INCOME	$ _____

Rentals and Other Income

RENTALS

This account should be credited with the income from rentals of space for business purposes. The account may be subdivided according to the following captions:

Stores

The rent income from space in the property used for stores.

Offices

The rent income from space in the motel/hotel building used as offices by tenants other than concessionaires.

Clubs

The rent income from space in the small hotel or motel building used as club rooms. Direct expenses of the small hotel or motel in connection with such club rooms, i.e., expenses of the same nature as are charged to the rooms department, should be charged to this account.

Others

The rent income from lobby space, show cases and all other space except that classified as offices, clubs, stores, and concessions.

Commissions to renting agents should be charged against the gross income from rentals under each classification. The schedule may include only the net rentals, or preferably the gross rentals, commissions, and expenses and the resulting net rentals.

CONCESSIONS

This account should be credited with the revenue received from others for the privilege of operating departments which might be operated by the property itself as part of the usual service.

Expenses to the small hotel or motel in connection with the operation of a concession (which would be charged as departmental expenses if the department were operated by the property) should be charged against the income received from the concessionaire.

COMMISSIONS

This account should be credited with the commissions received from laundry, valet, and other, including auto rentals, garage and parking lot, photographs, radio, taxicab, telegraph, and television. If a telegraph company occupies space in the lobby, the income to the property from such space should be credited to rentals even though the income is determined on the percentage basis. Similarly, so-called commissions from concessionaires should be included in the income from concessions.

INTEREST INCOME

This account should be credited with interest earned on bank deposits, notes receivable, and from other sources. There are situations, however, where contractual arrangements between small hotel or motel owners and operators specify that interest income should not be included in operating income. Where these circumstances exist, it would be appropriate to report interest income separately, as a line item below "Income before income taxes and gain or loss on sale of property" in the Statement of Income.

VENDING MACHINES

The revenue derived from vending machines, less the cost of merchandise sold, should be credited to this account, classified as desired.

CASH DISCOUNTS EARNED

This account should be credited with the discount earned by the payment of creditors' accounts within the discount period, but should not be credited with trade discounts which are more properly a deduction from cost of goods sold.

SALVAGE

Revenue derived from the sale of waste paper, incidental articles or obsolete materials, should be credited to this account.

MISCELLANEOUS

Under this classification should be grouped incidental items not distributable under previous captions.

Schedule B-7

ADMINISTRATIVE AND GENERAL EXPENSES

	Current Period
SALARIES AND WAGES	$
EMPLOYEE BENEFITS	
Total Payroll and Related Expenses	_____
OTHER EXPENSES	
Commission on Credit Card Charges — Net	
Data Processing Expense	
Insurance — General	
Licenses and Dues	
Management Fees	
Miscellaneous	
Postage and Telegrams	
Printing and Stationery	
Professional Fees	
Provision for Doubtful Accounts	
Security	
Trade Association Dues and Trade Publications	
Traveling Expenses	_____
Total Other Expenses	_____
TOTAL ADMINISTRATIVE AND GENERAL EXPENSES	$_____

Administrative and General Expenses

SALARIES AND WAGES

For the classification of employees included in this group, see administrative and general payroll schedule, page 72.

EMPLOYEE BENEFITS

This account is charged with vacation and holiday pay and the allocated portion of payroll taxes and social insurance and other related expenses properly applicable to this department. The cost of food and beverage furnished to employees, and other amounts such as Christmas bonus and severance pay, are also included in this account.

OTHER EXPENSES

*Commission on Credit Card Charges — Net

This account is charged with the amount of commissions paid to credit card organizations. Volume rebate payments received from credit card organizations should be credited to this account.

Data Processing Expense

The cost of data processing services, other than rental of equipment, should be charged to this expense.

Insurance — General

The proportion of all insurance premiums (exclusive of workmen's compensation insurance, fire insurance on buildings and contents, and social insurance as provided for on page 66) should be charged to this account, including the following:

Boiler liability	Fraud	Products liability
Burglary	Holdup	Property damage
Elevator liability	Life insurance	Public liability
Fidelity bonds	Lost and damaged	Robbery
Flywheel liability	goods	Use and occupancy
Forgery		

*When these amounts are substantial and are primarily incurred for sales purposes, notation of the amounts applicable to the various operating departments, particularly Rooms and Food and Beverage, should be made on the respective schedules.

Licenses and Dues

This account should be charged with federal, state, or municipal licenses which cannot be charged directly to the operations of a particular department. Also under this heading is included the cost of representation of the establishment in business organizations, not of a directly promotional nature, or of members of the staff when authorized to represent the property.

Management Fees

Fees charged by a management organization for management service or supervision should be charged to this account.

Miscellaneous

Under this classification should be grouped items not distributable under other captions, including the following:

Carfare
Cash overage & shortage
Christmas expenses
Contributions and donations,
    other than promotional
Credit and collection expenses
Exchange on bank checks
Executive office expenses
Express and freight charges not
    provided for elsewhere

Internal communication systems
Loss and damages
Mail bags
Paper towels for employees
Protective service cost
Safe-deposit box rental
Storage of equipment
Trustees' and registrars' fees
Uniforms

Postage and Telegrams

This account should be charged with the cost of postage, telegrams, and cables, except amounts applicable to marketing.

Printing and Stationery

The cost of printed forms, service manuals, stationery, and office supplies should be charged to this account when used by the manager's office, the accounting office, or by employees whose salaries and wages are charged to this group of expenses, as designated by the payroll schedule, page 72. The following list indicates the nature of the items to be included in this account.

Adding machine paper	Fountain pens	Pencils
Bank checks	Guest ledgers	Pens
Billing machine supplies	Ink	Pins
	Ink pads	Report covers
Binders	Ink wells	Rubber bands
Blotters	Mucilage	Rubber stamps
Books of account	Office supplies	Stamp pads
Books — record	Paper clips	Staples
Carbon paper	Paste	Stationery
Clips	Pen holders	Transcripts
Envelopes	Pen points	Typewriter ribbons

Professional Fees

The cost of attorneys, public accountants, and professional consultants, including fees, travel expenses, and maintenance, should be charged to this account.

Provision for Doubtful Accounts

A monthly charge adequate to provide for the probable loss in collection of motel accounts receivable should be charged to this account, with the contra entry a credit to the allowance for doubtful accounts.

Security

The cost of providing security for guests, personnel, and property should be charged to this account, including alarm, armored car, and guard services.

Trade Association Dues and Trade Publications

The cost of representation of the property in business organizations and subscriptions to papers, magazines, and books for use of personnel should be charged to this account.

Traveling Expenses

The cost of maintenance and transportation of officers and employees of the establishment, traveling on business, should be charged to this account, except that traveling in connection with business promotion should be charged to "Marketing."

MARKETING

	Current Period
SALES	$
Salaries and Wages	
Employee Benefits	
Total Payroll and Related Expenses	_____
Other Selling Expenses	
Total Sales	_____
ADVERTISING	
Other Advertising Expenses	
Outdoor	
Print	
Radio and Television	
Total Advertising	_____
MERCHANDISING	_____
PUBLIC RELATIONS AND PUBLICITY	_____
RESEARCH	_____
FEES AND COMMISSIONS	
Agency Fees	
Franchise Fees	
Other Fees and Commissions	
Total Fees and Commissions	_____
OTHER SELLING AND PROMOTION EXPENSES	_____
TOTAL MARKETING	$ _____

Marketing

This group of accounts should be charged with all costs incurred in connection with the creation and maintenance of the image of the small hotel or motel and the development, promotion, and furtherance of new business.

Where long-term contracts are entered into for advertising or for any of the other marketing expenses, the cost should be prorated over the term of the contract, and the unexpired portion shown as a deferred asset in the balance sheet.

The following accounts are given as examples, and should be followed as closely as possible; however, these may be condensed or expanded to suit the requirements of the particular property.

SALES

Salaries and Wages

For the classification of employees included in this group, see marketing payroll schedule, page 72.

Employee Benefits

This account is charged with vacation and holiday pay and the allocated portion of payroll taxes and social insurance and the other related expenses properly applicable to this department. The cost of food and beverages furnished to department employees, and other amounts such as Christmas bonus and severance pay, are also included in this account.

Other Selling Expenses

The costs to be charged to this account include the following:

Operating supplies
  Office supplies
  Printed forms
  Sales manuals
  Stationery

Postage
Telegrams
Trade show expense
  Rental of exhibition space
  Travel and subsistence
Travel and entertainment

ADVERTISING

Other Advertising Expenses

Any advertising not charged to the specific accounts provided for advertising should be charged to this account.

Outdoor

The cost of poster or painted billboards and other signs should be charged to this account including the regular monthly charges for service and rental.

Print

Newspaper, magazine, and directory advertising costs should be charged to this category.

Radio and Television

The cost of advertising on radio and television should be charged to this account, including the cost of production.

MERCHANDISING

All costs incurred to merchandise the services of the small hotel or motel should be recorded in this account. The costs to be included are as follows:

In-house graphics
  Directories
  Signs
  Brochures
Selling aids
  Salespersons' kits
  Maps
  Floor plans

Point of sale material
  Spiral tent cards
  Menu flyers
  Wine

PUBLIC RELATIONS AND PUBLICITY

All costs incurred relative to public relations and publicity should be recorded in this account. This includes the cost of convention bureau activities, contributions to specific or general convention funds, fees paid to public relations representatives or agencies, and the cost of photographs used in promotional programs.

RESEARCH

The costs related to marketing research should be recorded in this account.

FEES AND COMMISSIONS

Agency Fees

This account includes any advertising agency retainer fees and special fees.

Franchise Fees

All fees charged by the franchise company including royalty fees and those for national advertising should be charged to this account.

Other Fees and Commissions

This includes all other marketing fees and commissions not classified elsewhere.

OTHER SELLING AND PROMOTION EXPENSES

All other marketing not classified elsewhere should be recorded in this account. This includes such costs as membership fees paid for employees of the marketing department and expenses associated with the provision of complimentary services to guests which arise from selling and promotional activities.

Schedule B-9

PROPERTY OPERATION, MAINTENANCE, AND ENERGY COSTS

	Current Period
SALARIES AND WAGES	$
EMPLOYEE BENEFITS	
Total Payroll and Related Expenses	_____
OTHER EXPENSES	
Building	
Electrical and Mechanical Equipment	
Engineering Supplies	
Furniture, Fixtures, Equipment and Decor	
Grounds and Landscaping	
Miscellaneous	
Operating Supplies	
Removal of Waste Matter	
Uniforms	_____
Total	_____
TOTAL PROPERTY OPERATION AND MAINTENANCE	_____
ENERGY COSTS	
Electric Current	
Fuel	
Steam	
Water	
Total Energy Costs	_____
TOTAL PROPERTY OPERATION, MAINTENANCE AND ENERGY COSTS	$_____

Property Operation, Maintenance, and Energy Costs

SALARIES AND WAGES

For the classification of employees in this group, see property operation and maintenance payroll schedule, page 72.

EMPLOYEE BENEFITS

This account is charged with vacation and holiday pay and the allocated portion of payroll taxes and social insurance and other related expenses properly applicable to this department. The cost of food and beverage furnished to employees included in property operation and maintenance, and other amounts such as Christmas bonus and severance pay, are also included in this account.

OTHER EXPENSES

Building

Supplies

This account should be charged with the cost of material used in repairing the building, both interior and exterior, including the following:

Ceilings	Masonry	Walls
Doors	Plaster	Waterproofing
Fire escapes	Roof	Windows
Fire hose	Sidewalks	
Floors	Stairways	

Contracts

This account should include only the cost of work let to outside concerns, including sandblasting.

Electrical and Mechanical Equipment

This account should be charged with the cost of materials used in repairing equipment. The proper subclassifications should be charged if subclassifications are used; namely, air conditioning and refrigeration, general electrical and mechanical equipment, kitchen equipment, laundry equipment, plumbing and heating, and elevators.

Engineering Supplies

This account should be charged with the supplies used in the engineer's department, including the following:

Fuses	Packing	Water treatment
Greases	Solvents	chemicals and
Oils	Waste	additives

Furniture, Fixtures, Equipment, and Decor

This account should be charged for the cost of materials to repair the following:

Curtains and draperies

Floor coverings for guest rooms, corridors,
   dining rooms, and public rooms

Furniture

Further, this account should be charged with the cost of materials and supplies for painting and decorating.

Grounds and Landscaping

Maintenance of grounds should be charged to this account.

Miscellaneous

Under this classification should be grouped such items as are not distributable under other captions, including cost of laboratory tests, licenses and meter rentals.

Operating Supplies

The cost of cleaning supplies, electric bulbs, printing and stationery, and other similar items for use in property operation and maintenance should be charged to this account.

Removal of Waste Matter

The cost of the removal of rubbish and of operating an incinerator should be charged to this account.

Uniforms

The charges to this account should be handled in the same general manner as described in the account of similar title in the rooms department schedule, page 30.

ENERGY COSTS

Electric Current

The cost of light and power purchased from outside producers, including cost of breakdown service, should be charged to this account.

Fuel

This account should include the cost of fuel consumed, except kitchen fuel charged to the Food and Beverage department. The type of fuel used, such as coal, oil or gas, should be stated.

Steam

The cost of steam puchased from outside producers should be charged to this account.

Water

This account should be charged with the cost of water consumed and should include water especially treated for a circulating ice water system or purchased for drinking purposes.

60

RENT, PROPERTY TAXES AND OTHER MUNICIPAL CHARGES, AND INSURANCE

	Current Period
RENT	
Real Estate (Land and Buildings)	$
Furnishings, Fixtures and Equipment	
Electronic Data Processing Equipment	
Other Rentals	_____
Total Rent	_____
PROPERTY TAXES AND OTHER MUNICIPAL CHARGES	
Real Estate Taxes	
Personal Property Taxes	
Utility Taxes	
Business and Occupation Taxes	
Other	_____
Total Property Taxes and Other Municipal Charges	_____
INSURANCE ON BUILDING AND CONTENTS	_____
TOTAL RENT, PROPERTY TAXES AND OTHER MUNICIPAL CHARGES, AND INSURANCE	$ _____

INTEREST EXPENSE

Notes Payable	$
First Mortgage	
Other Long-Term Debt	
Other Interest	
Amortization of Deferred Financing Costs	_____
Total Interest Expense	$ _____

DEPRECIATION AND AMORTIZATION

DEPRECIATION	
Building and Improvements	$
Furnishings, Fixtures and Equipment	
Other	
AMORTIZATION	
Leaseholds and Improvements	
Preopening Expenses	
Other	_____
Total Depreciation and Amortization	$ _____
GAIN OR LOSS ON SALE OF PROPERTY, NET	$ _____

(continued)

FEDERAL AND STATE INCOME TAXES

FEDERAL
    Deferred
    Current
        Total Federal   ————

STATE
    Deferred
    Current
        Total State   ————

TOTAL FEDERAL AND STATE INCOME TAXES $ ————

Rent, Property Taxes and Other Municipal Charges, and Insurance

RENT

Real Estate

If the property is leased, this account should be charged with the amount of the rental of the property showing separately, if material, the rental cost for the real estate and the rental costs for the furnishings, fixtures, and equipment.

Electronic Data Processing

The account should also be charged with the rental cost of electronic data processing equipment which, if material, should also be stated separately.

Other Rentals

Other rentals would include the cost of the rental of any other major items which, had they not been rented, would be purchased and capitalized as fixed assets, except telephone equipment.

Rental of miscellaneous equipment (copiers, projectors, or sound equipment) for a specific function, such as a banquet or similar function, should be charged to the appropriate department and would not be considered rental expense chargeable to this account.

PROPERTY TAXES AND OTHER MUNICIPAL CHARGES

Real Estate Taxes

This account should be charged with all taxes assessed against the real property of the small hotel or motel by a state or political subdivision of a state, such as a county or city. Assessments for public improvements are not to be included in this account as they should be capitalized as a fixed asset.

Personal Property Taxes

Personal property taxes should also be charged to this account and, if material, should be shown separately.

Utility Taxes

Taxes assessed by utilities, such as sewer taxes, should be charged to this account. Normal charges for refuse removal and utility services would be charged to property operation and maintenance.

Business and Occupation Taxes

Business and occupation taxes, such as gross receipts taxes on sale of rooms, food and beverage that cannot be passed along to customers, should be charged to this account.

Other Taxes

Any other taxes, other than income and payroll taxes, would be charged to "other" taxes and separately identified if material.

INSURANCE ON BUILDING AND CONTENTS

The cost of insuring the buildings and contents against damage or destruction by fire, weather, sprinkler leakage, boiler explosion, plate glass breakage, or any other cause should be charged to this account.

INTEREST EXPENSE

This account should be charged with all interest expense on any obligation, such as notes payable, first mortgages, second mortgages, bonds, debentures, taxes in arrears or any other indebtedness on which interest is charged. Amortization of deferred financing costs and other costs related to obtaining financing should be charged to this account over the estimated period of the related financing. Interest charges should be grouped into categories which indicate the source of the principal indebtedness on which interest is incurred.

DEPRECIATION AND AMORTIZATION

Depreciation

Buildings and improvements

Depreciation on the buildings and improvements should be charged to this account over the estimated useful life of the building or related improvement.

Furniture, Fixtures, and Equipment

Depreciation of furniture, fixtures, and equipment should be charged to this account over their estimated life. The account is not to include depreciation of china, glassware, silver, linen, and uniforms when such items are accounted for by the inventory method and charged to the particular department using the equipment. In cases where such equipment is amortized or depreciated, it should be charged to this account.

Amortization

The amortization of the costs of acquiring a leasehold and leasehold improvements should be charged to this account over the life of the related lease or, in the case of improvements, over the life of the improvement if less than that of the related lease. The account should also be charged with the amortization of preopening expenditures if such expenditures are capitalized. Generally, amortization of preopening expenditures would be over a relatively short period of time.

GAIN OR LOSS ON SALE OF PROPERTY NET

Gains or losses from the sale of property should be combined and stated separately if significant. If such gains or losses are not significant, they should be shown as a separate line category in the Rentals and Other Income schedule B-6.

FEDERAL AND STATE INCOME TAXES

All taxes which are assessed on the basis of the income earned by the enterprise should be charged to this account.

When there are differences between income reported for financial statement purposes and income reported for income tax purposes, the amount of income tax currently payable and the amount which has been deferred should be shown separately. Items which give rise to deferred income taxes include, but are not limited to, the difference in tax and book depreciation and items capitalized as fixed assets on the books but treated as expense for tax purposes.

Allocated Departments

(Memorandum schedules of fully allocated cost centers or departments)

The schedules that follow contain the details of the fully allocated expense departments:

Employee benefits
House laundry
Salaries and wages

The bases of allocation should be shown in each schedule.

Schedule B-11

EMPLOYEE BENEFITS

	Current Period
PAYROLL TAXES	$
Federal Retirement	
Federal Unemployment	
State Unemployment	
Total Payroll Taxes	___
SOCIAL INSURANCE	___
Non-Union Insurance	
Non-Union Pension	
State Health Insurance	
Union Insurance	
Union Pension	
Workmen's Compensation Insurance	
Other	
Total Social Insurance	___
OTHER EXPENSES	___
Miscellaneous	
TOTAL EMPLOYEE BENEFITS	$ ___

CHARGED TO DEPARTMENTS		
Rooms	Schedule B-1	
Food and Beverages	Schedule B-2	
Telephone	Schedule B-3	
Gift Shop	Schedule B-4	
Gas Station — Garage — Parking	Schedule B-5	
Administrative and General	Schedule B-7	
Marketing	Schedule B-8	
Property Operations, Maintenance, and Energy Costs	Schedule B-9	
House Laundry	Schedule B-12	___
TOTAL EMPLOYEE BENEFITS		$ ___

Employee Benefits

PAYROLL TAXES

Federal Retirement Tax (FICA)

This account to be charged with taxes imposed on employees by Subchapter B, Chapter 21 of the Internal Revenue Code.

Federal Unemployment Tax (FUTA)

This account to be charged with taxes imposed by Chapter 23 of the Internal Revenue Code.

State Unemployment Tax

This account to be charged with contributions by employers to unemployment funds required by unemployment compensation laws of the various states.

SOCIAL INSURANCE

Non-Union Insurance

Contributions or premiums paid into non-union employees' benefit fund for insurance on life, health, accident, hospitalization, and other purposes.

Non-Union Pension

Contributions or premiums paid for the pension funds, or combination pension and insurance fund contributions.

State Health Insurance

Amounts paid to taxing authorities or to insurance companies for health insurance coverage should be charged to this account.

Union Insurance

Contributions or premiums paid into union employees' benefit funds for insurance on life, health, accident, hospitalization, and other purposes.

Union Pension

Contributions or premiums paid for the pension funds or combination pension and insurance fund contributions.

Workmen's Compensation Insurance

This account to be charged with the workmen's compensation and employer's liability insurance premiums.

OTHER EXPENSES

Miscellaneous

Under this classification should be grouped items that pertain to the benefit of the employees, but are not chargeable under other captions. This may include physicians' fees, medical supplies, and awards as well as the costs of any social functions for the benefit of the employees.

Schedule B-12

HOUSE LAUNDRY

		Current Period
SALARIES AND WAGES		$
EMPLOYEE BENEFITS		
Total Payroll and Related Expenses		
OTHER EXPENSES		
Cleaning Supplies		
Laundry Supplies		
Miscellaneous		
Printing and Stationery		
Uniforms		
Total Expenses		
CREDITS		
Cost of Guest Laundry		
Cost of Concessionaires' Laundry		
Total Credits		
COST OF HOUSE LAUNDRY		$
CHARGED TO —		
Rooms	Schedule B-1	$
Food & Beverages	Schedule B-2	
Other Departments	Schedule B-	
Total		$

House Laundry

SALARIES AND WAGES

For the classification of employees included in this group, see house laundry payroll schedule, page 72.

EMPLOYEE BENEFITS

This account is charged with vacation and holiday pay and the allocated portion of payroll taxes and social insurance and other related expenses properly applicable to this department. The cost of food and beverage furnished to employees included in this department, and other amounts such as Christmas bonus and severance pay, are also included in this account.

OTHER EXPENSES

Cleaning Supplies

The charges to this account should be handled in the same general manner as described in the account of similar title in the Rooms Department schedule, page 29. This account should not include materials used for laundering purposes provided for below.

Laundry Supplies

The items to be included in this group are suggested by the following:

Acids	Duck	Shirt bands
Aprons for mangles	Ecru	Shirt fronts
Bags	Erusticator	Soaps
Bluing	Felt padding	Soda
Boxes	Laundry bags	Starch
Buttons	Marking ink	Tags
Cardboard	Oxalic acid	Twine
Chemicals	Pins	Wrapping paper
Chloride of Lime	Salt	

Miscellaneous

Under this classification should be grouped items not chargeable under other captions.

Printing and Stationery

The cost of printed forms, service manuals, stationery, and office supplies should be charged to this account, including laundry lists.

Uniforms

The charges to this account should be handled in the same general manner as described in the account of similar title in the Rooms Department schedule, page 30.

CREDITS

Cost of Guest Laundry

Where no separate guest laundry is maintained, this account should be credited with 60 percent of the total revenue derived from work done for guests and outside parties. If the experience of the operation proves that 60 percent is greater or less than the approximate cost of guest work, the percentage should be adjusted accordingly.

Cost of Concessionaires' Laundry

Where laundering is done for concessionaires, the revenue received usually contains little or no profit; therefore, the entire revenue should be deducted from the departmental expenses.

COST OF HOUSE LAUNDRY

The cost of house laundry should be distributed to rooms, food and beverage, and other departments on a percentage, pound, or count basis.

SALARIES AND WAGES

	Current Period	
	Number of Employees	Amount
ROOMS		
Assistant managers		$
Front Office		
Housekeeping		
Housekeeper and Assistants		
Linen Room		
Maids		
Housemen		
Night Cleaners		
Window Cleaners		
Service		
Front		
Elevators		
Floors		
Doormen		
Package Room and Baggage Porters		
Miscellaneous		
House Officers and Watchmen		
Total		$
Less: Charged to Other Departments		
Assistant Managers		
Linen Room		
Housemen		
Night Cleaners		
Window Cleaners		
Elevator Service		
House Offices and Watchmen		
Total Charge to Other Departments		
Total Rooms (Schedule B-1)		$

(continued)

Salaries and Wages

| | Current Period | |
	Number of Employees	Amount
FOOD AND BEVERAGE		
Food Preparation		$
Chefs and Assistants		
Cooks		
Pot Washer (Cook's Helpers)		
Butcher		
Vegetable Cleaners		
Pastry		
Bakery		
Ice Cream		
Pantry, Oyster, Coffee		
Miscellaneous		
Food Service		
Restaurants		
Managers, Hostesses, Head Waiters, Captains		
Waiters and Waitresses		
Busboys		
Room Service		
Headwaiters and Captains		
Waiters and Waitresses		
Bus Boys		
Order Clerks		
Banquet		
Maitre d'Hotel, Banquet Manager and Assistants		
Headwaiters and Captains		
Waiters and Waitresses		
Banquet Housemen		
Charges from other Departments		
Beverage Service		
Bartenders		
Barboys		
Hostesses, Headwaiters and Captains		
Waiters and Waitresses		
Employees' Dining Rooms		
Food and Beverage — General		
Cashiers, Checkers		
Food and Beverage Control		
Stewards and Assistants		
Storekeepers		
Purchasing		
Warewashing and Cleaning		
Miscellaneous		
Total Food and Beverage (Schedule B-2)		$

72

Schedule B-13
(continued)

Salaries and Wages

	Current Period	
	Number of Employees	Amount
TELEPHONE		
Chief Operator		$
Operators	_____	_____
Total (Schedule B-3)	_____	_____
GIFT SHOP		
Manager		
Sales Clerks		
Cashiers		
Other	_____	_____
Total (Schedule B-4)	_____	_____
GAS STATION — GARAGE — PARKING		
Manager		
Attendants		
Mechanics	_____	_____
Total (Schedule B-5)	_____	_____
OTHER OPERATED DEPARTMENTS		
(Schedule B-)	_____	_____
ADMINISTRATIVE AND GENERAL		
Manager and Manager's Office		
Accounting		
Payroll	_____	_____
Total (Schedule B-7)	_____	_____
MARKETING (Schedule B-8)	_____	_____
PROPERTY OPERATION, MAINTENANCE, AND ENERGY COSTS		
Chief Engineer		
Engineers		
Carpenter and Furniture Repairer		
Painters and Paperhangers		
General Mechanics		
Electricians		
Plumbers		
Grounds and Landscaping		
Other	_____	_____
Total (Schedule B-9)	_____	_____
HOUSE LAUNDRY		
Manager		
Washing and Finishing		
Other	_____	_____
Total (Schedule B-12)	_____	_____
TOTAL SALARIES AND WAGES	_____	$ _____

SECTION IV

Statement of Changes in Financial Position and Notes to Financial Statements

The financial presentation, in addition to the Balance Sheet and Statement of Income, should include a Statement of Changes in Financial Position. The purpose of this statement is to summarize the financing and investing activities of the entity, including the extent to which it has generated funds from operations during the period, and to complete the disclosure of changes in financial position during the period.

The Statement should prominently disclose working capital or cash provided from or used in operations for the period, with the effect of extraordinary items being reported separately. The statement for the period should begin with income or loss before extraordinary items, if any, and add back (or deduct) items recognized in determining that income or loss which did not use (or provide) working capital or cash during the period. This should be followed by working capital or cash provided or used by income or loss from extraordinary items, if any. Extraordinary income or loss should be similarly adjusted for items recognized that did not provide or use working capital or cash during the period. Net changes in each element of working capital as customarily defined should be disclosed.

In addition to working capital or cash provided from operations, including extraordinary items, and changes in elements of working capital, the Statement should also disclose changes resulting from purchase and sale of long-term assets, issuance or redemption of debt or equity obligations or securities, dividends and other similar transactions.

A detailed format for the Statement of Changes in Financial Position is shown in Exhibit C on the following page.

Exhibit C

STATEMENT OF CHANGES IN FINANCIAL POSITION

	Period Ending	
	19 _____	19 _____
SOURCE OF FUNDS		
Net Income	$	$
Items Which Did Not Affect Working Capital		
Depreciation and Amortization		
Writeoff (deferral) of Preopening and		
Other Business Development Expenses		
Deferred Income Taxes		
Other — Net	_____	_____
Working Capital Provided from Operations		
Disposition of Property and Equipment		
Proceeds from Long-term Borrowings		
Issuance of Equity Securities		
Other — Net		
Working Capital Provided	_____	_____
USE OF FUNDS		
Additions to Property and Equipment		
Additions to Investments and Advances		
Purchase of Treasury Stock		
Reduction of Long-term Debt		
Dividends Paid		
Other — Net	_____	_____
Working Capital Used	_____	_____
INCREASE (DECREASE) IN WORKING CAPITAL	$ _____	$ _____
SUMMARY OF CHANGES IN WORKING CAPITAL:		
Cash	$	$
Accounts and Notes Receivable		
Other Current Assets		
Inventories		
Current Maturities on Long-term Debt		
Accounts Payable and Accrued Liabilities		
Accrued Taxes		
Other Current Liabilities	_____	_____
INCREASE (DECREASE) IN WORKING CAPITAL	$ _____	$ _____

See accompanying notes to financial statements.

THE STATEMENT OF CHANGES
IN FINANCIAL POSITION ILLUSTRATED

In order to prepare a Statement of Changes in Financial Position, hereinafter simply referred to as "Statement," the financial information required is as follows:

1. Balance Sheets for the beginning and end of the period.

2. Statement of Income for the period.

3. Details of changes in noncurrent Balance Sheet accounts.

To prepare the Statement, a five-step approach is recommended as follows:

1. Determine the working capital at the beginning and end of the period.

2. Determine the change in working capital for the period.

3. Determine the sources and uses of funds from analyzing the Statement of Income for the period.

4. Determine the sources and uses of funds from analyzing the noncurrent Balance Sheet account.

5. Prepare the Statement.

The five-step approach will be used to illustrate the preparation of the Statement for the Sample Motel. The comparative Balance Sheets for the Sample Motel are as follows:

SAMPLE MOTEL
BALANCE SHEET

	Beginning of Year	End of Year
CURRENT ASSETS:		
Cash	$ 5,000	$ 4,500
Accounts Receivable	10,000	12,000
Food Inventory	2,000	2,000
Prepaid Expenses	2,000	1,500
Total	19,000	20,000
PROPERTY AND EQUIPMENT:		
Furniture and Fixtures	40,000	48,000
Accumulated Depreciation, Furniture and Fixtures	(30,000)	(25,000)
Building	400,000	400,000
Accumulated Depreciation Building	(300,000)	(307,000)
Land	50,000	50,000
Total	160,000	166,000
Total Assets	$ 179,000	$ 186,000
CURRENT LIABILITIES:		
Accounts Payable	$ 7,000	$ 6,000
Wages Payable	2,000	2,000
Total	9,000	8,000
NONCURRENT LIABILITIES:		
Mortgage Payable	100,000	95,000
Note — Local Bank	-0-	7,000
Total	100,000	102,000
SHAREHOLDERS' EQUITY:		
Capital Stock	10,000	10,000
Retained Earnings	60,000	66,000
Total	70,000	76,000
Total Liabilities and Stockholders' Equity	$ 179,000	$ 186,000

SAMPLE MOTEL
STATEMENT OF INCOME

	Revenue	Cost of Sales	Related Expenses	Payroll and Other Expenses	Income (Loss)
Rooms	$120,000	$ -0-	$30,000	$30,000	$60,000
Food	50,000	20,000	15,000	8,000	7,000
Rentals and Other Income	10,000	-0-	-0-	-0-	10,000
Total	180,000	20,000	45,000	38,000	77,000
Undistributed Operating Expenses:					
Administrative and General			20,000	2,000	22,000
Marketing			-0-	5,000	5,000
Property Operation, Maintenance and Energy Costs			5,000	15,000	20,000
Total	$180,000	$20,000	$70,000	$60,000	47,000

Total Income Before Fixed Charges	30,000
Rent, Property Taxes and Insurance	7,000
Interest Expense	5,000
Depreciation Expense	10,000
Total Income Before Gain on Sale of Property and Income Taxes	8,000
Gain on Sale of Property	2,000
Income Before Income Taxes	10,000
Income Taxes	3,000
Net Income	$ 7,000

Other information required for preparation of the example Statement is as follows:

1. During the year various furniture items costing $10,000 with a net book value of $2,000 were sold for $4,000 resulting in a gain on the sale of $2,000.

2. Dividends declared and paid during the year totaled $1,000.

3. Furniture purchased during the year cost $18,000. Seven thousand dollars were borrowed from a local bank to partially finance the purchase. The amount borrowed is payable in full at the end of three years.

4. The mortgage payment during the year reduced the principal amount of the loan by $5,000.

5. The food operation (coffee shop) sold 12,000 covers during the year, while 6,000 rooms were sold. (This information is provided to illustrate ratio analysis, later in the book.)

FIVE-STEP APPROACH ILLUSTRATED

STEP 1 — Determine working capital

	Beginning of Year	End of Year
Current Assets	$ 19,000	$ 20,000
Current Liabilities	9,000	8,000
Working Capital	$ 10,000	$12,000

STEP 2 — Determine change in working capital

Working Capital — end of year	$ 12,000
Working Capital — beginning of year	(10,000)
Change in Working Capital (Increase)	$ 2,000

STEP 3 — Analyze the Statement of Income

Net Income	= $	7,000	(source)
Depreciation	=	10,000	(show in source section)
Gain on Sale of Property	=	2,000	(show proceeds from sale of $4,000 as a separate source)

STEP 4 — Analyze noncurrent accounts in Balance Sheet

Furniture and Fixtures	— (use — purchased $18,000)
Mortgage Payable	— (use — reduced principal $5,000)
Note — Local Bank	— (source — borrowed $7,000)
Retained Earnings	— (source — net income $7,000; use — dividend $1,000)

STEP 5 — Prepare Statement (See next page)

SAMPLE MOTEL
STATEMENT OF CHANGES IN FINANCIAL POSITION

SOURCE OF FUNDS

Net income	$ 7,000
Items which did not offset working capital	
Depreciation	10,000
Gain on sale of furniture	(2,000)
Working capital provided from operations	15,000
Proceeds from sale of furniture	4,000
Proceeds from note — local bank	7,000
Working capital provided	26,000

USE OF FUNDS

Additions to furniture	18,000
Dividends paid	1,000
Reduction of mortgage payable	5,000
Working capital used	24,000
Increase (Decrease) in Working Capital	$ 2,000

SUMMARY OF CHANGES IN WORKING CAPITAL:

Cash	$ (500)
Accounts Receivable	2,000
Prepaid Expenses	(500)
Accounts Payable	1,000
INCREASE (DECREASE) IN WORKING CAPITAL	$2,000

A comparative Statement of Changes in Financial Position should be included in the financial presentation when comparative Statements of Income are provided. For illustrative purposes, the Statement of Changes in Financial Position is shown only for one year.

NOTES TO FINANCIAL STATEMENTS

The financial presentation, to be complete, should normally include explanatory Notes to the Financial Statements.

There should be included in the notes a description of all significant accounting policies followed by the reporting entity. Commonly required disclosures include, but are not limited to, policies relating to:

a. Basis of consolidation
b. Depreciation methods
c. Accounting for investments
d. Amortization of intangibles
e. Inventory pricing
f. Pension profit sharing and/or stock option plans
g. Recognition of income from franchising or leasing operations
h. Accounting for deferred business development costs, including preopening expense, and other deferred charges

   i. Computation of net income per share
   j. Amortization of the cost in excess of net assets of businesses acquired
   k. Accounting for income taxes

This section should be followed by such additional notes as are necessary to provide for full disclosure of all significant events or conditions reflected in the financial statements, or as otherwise required by the rules of professional accounting or regulatory organizations.

Typical items with respect to which all significant facts, if material in nature, should be disclosed through such notes are the following:

   a. Long term debt agreements
   b. Leases
   c. Contingent liabilities
   d. Pending lawsuits
   e. Pension and/or profit sharing plans
   f. Income taxes
   g. Changes in accounting methods
   h. Long term contracts
   i. Stock options
   j. Extraordinary items of income or expense

SECTION V

Included in this section are suggested procedures relating to the following:

1. Budgeting and Forecasting
2. Uniform Account Numbering System
3. Ratio Analysis

They are included for illustrative purposes and for general guidance of the reader in these matters.

Budgeting and Forecasting

In the extremely competitive environment of the small hotel/motel business, the importance of budgeting and forecasting cannot be overemphasized. At the local level it provides the opportunity for management to appraise the overall operation for the coming year through an evaluation of the property's strengths and weaknesses, and to plan operating strategies to capitalize on or counteract these, as the case may be. Where the property is a member of an affiliated group, the budget is essential to headquarters management in the development of overall company financial and operating policies. Consequently, the system of accounts is designed in such a way as to accommodate the budgeting and forecasting process. This is accomplished through the forms of statements used in presenting results of operations, principally Statements of Income and Changes in Financial Position, together with any back-up or supporting schedules that may be desired.

There are three basic elements in completing the annual budgeting and forecasting cycle:

1. Preparation of the Budget
2. Operation of the Budget
3. Forms of Statements

PREPARATION OF THE BUDGET
General

The work involved in preparation of the budget (or plan) requires a closely coordinated effort of all supervisory and management personnel in the property. Each person who has the responsibility for running a department or activity in the property should participate in the preparation of the budget. The property's accounting department normally would have the responsibility for coordinating preparation of the budget, preparation of statistical information on previous performance, labor or current or agreed-upon salary rates, tax information, maintenance program status, and other essential data. The general manager should generally have over-all responsibility for the preparation and content of the budget and, while he/she may delegate the responsibility for its preparation, he/she will usually be expected to assume responsibility for its content.

Prior to commencement of detailed work on preparation of the budget, a list of assumptions on which it will be based should be prepared. This will serve as a guide to those preparing various sections of the budget as to factors to be considered, and it will also provide a means for analyzing the causes for variances between budgeted and actual results during the budget year. A discussion of the various factors which should be considered in developing such a list is included in this section.

Time Schedule

In order to insure that adequate time is available for preparation of a budget and review and approval by management or owners, a time schedule should be set and closely followed.

A schedule somewhat like the following could be recommended for a calendar year company:

Budget Planning Meetings	October 20-31
Departmental Preparation Plan	November 1-9
Consolidation of Departmental Plans by Accounting	November 10-19
Review by General Manager and Preparation of Manager's Budget Report	November 20-30
Review by Owner (Board of Directors)	December

To meet such a schedule, the property supervisors and the general manager should have a preliminary outline of their budgets prepared before the budget planning meeting so that each individual will be in a position to discuss the broad scope of his/her proposed plan for the ensuing year. The accounting and statistical data that is to be maintained in the accounting department must be kept up-to-date each month and should be available as needed by the department supervisors and general manager as they prepare and discuss their budgets. In this way the planning work will be virtually a continuous process of comparing current operations to the budget on a monthly basis, examining variations from the budget, and recording information that will assist in preparation of the subsequent year's budget.

Budget Planning Meetings

A few months before the beginning of each year the property manager should call a meeting of his/her supervisory staff to perform the following work:

1. **Review current year's operations** — The property operations for the current year to date, which would represent from nine to ten months' operation for the property, should be reviewed by the manager and his/her staff to determine items of *continuing significance* that occurred during the year. These items might include rate changes, additions to facilities or reductions in existing facilities, major labor changes, improvements in efficiency that were implemented during the year, etc. This should include a thorough analysis of the principal causes of failure to meet current year budgeted results or of improvements over budget. The potential effect of such items on the budget year operations will need to be projected so that proper recognition can be given in establishing the statistical base for revenue and costs upon which the budget is to be built.

2. **General business and economic conditions** — General business conditions nationally and of the area of the small hotel or motel need to be ascertained to determine their effect on the budget year's operations. This requires an analysis of the current economic climate in the immediate area and projections for change during the budget year. The political and governmental climate should be considered, including a review of pending legislative changes, scheduled changes in existing laws, such as minimum wage rates, payroll taxes and similarities, and an evaluation made of their impact. Where substantial changes are indicated, the effect of these changes on the properties' operations must be projected. In addition, it is necessary to specify the action considered necessary to capitalize on any favorable economic climate or to offset an adverse climate. In order to provide a valid plan, the property manager must be in a position to interpolate general business and economic conditions into information usable in his own budget planning.

3. **Competitive situation** — The current competitive situation in the immediate area of the property needs to be ascertained in order to determine the effect of such competition on the budget. Competition from other properties should be given full recognition in projecting operating volumes. Where a small hotel or motel offers a wide variety of services, the competition in *each area* must also be separately analyzed. As an example, newly constructed properties or major renovations to existing properties may

have an impact on the competitive situation that must be recognized. The effect of new restaurants and other facilities must be given recognition. In each of these areas the person directly in charge of the individual property department should bring knowledge to the meeting on the potential problems and prospects in his/her area of responsibility. Here, as with economic conditions previously mentioned, the general manager and his/her staff must outline a plan of action to meet and/or overcome new competition and include the impact in the budget.

4. **Abnormal charges to operations** — Property management should review all abnormal charges to operations that affect the budget year. Abnormal charges are items of significance, such as unusual maintenance and repairs, changes in classifications of service, complete changes in linen, china, major capital items and so on. Each department in the property should be required to justify any abnormal items. When all potential charges have been identified and their effect on operations determined, the manager will determine which requests can be taken care of during the budget year and those which will have to be deferred until a later date or those which would require the borrowing of money. Such determinations cannot be settled until all interrelationships are reviewed and weighed to determine the overall impact on operations and finances for the budget year.

5. **Rates** — After review of the current year's operations, business conditions, competition and potential abnormal charges have been determined, the management group should review the rate structure of the property, including rooms, food and beverage, and all other services provided by the property. All rates should be reviewed to determine which rates will attract the volume of business necessary to best utilize the property's facilities. Such review should be primarily concerned with the maximum rates to be established to achieve maximum revenue. In effect the question to be answered is "What price or rate can be charged to achieve a maximum return from the facilities?" Obviously operating costs have a bearing. However, at this point in time the specific costs of operation will not be known and the determination as to whether or not rates should be changed will be based upon management's determination of the maximum rate obtainable without major reduction in volume.

During this process *each category* of rate in *each department* of the property should be reviewed and a determination made as to its adequacy and/or need for change within the budget year. If a change is indicated, further analysis should be undertaken to determine the specific changes (which rooms should be changed and how much, which meals and how much), and the timing required, including the lead time, to effect the change. Obviously it is essential that, where changes are to be made, they be made at the earliest possible time to insure that the property gets the benefit as quickly as possible.

6. **Occupancy and gross sales** — The projections for property occupancy should be divided into estimated *group business, individual business, walk-in business,* and so on, including permanent occupants, if any. These breakdowns are necessary in projecting percentages of occupancy by month for the budget year. The backlog of group bookings for the budget year should be carefully analyzed and considered in forecasting group occupancy percentages and average rates. Statistical information on group business should also be analyzed along with historic occupancy data in determining expected occupancies.

In a similar manner, food and beverage revenue should be projected. Projections can be broken into banquet and regular business. The banquet information should be available from catering records, with the balance coming from regular sources of food and beverage sales. Based upon projected occupancy and other relevant factors, other revenue sources such as garage, laundry, valet, and the like could also be projected so that a beginning estimate of total gross revenue is available.

At the conclusion of the budget planning meetings, the general outline of the plan, including occupancy and volume statistics, should be clearly defined. The effect of abnormal items on operations will have been determined and reflected in the projections. The next step in preparation of the budget requires each supervisory employee to refine the information that was made available at the budget planning meetings and prepare the specific detailed plan for his department or function.

Departmental Plan Preparation

Utilizing the information made available at the budget planning meetings, each department head should project the anticipated monthly activity for his/her area of responsibility. The estimate of revenue should be made based on these volume figures and the rate schedule that has been agreed upon at the budget planning meetings.

After the activity volume and revenue estimates have been determined, the costs of sales and operating expenses must be projected. The basic information to be used in making cost projections, such as salary schedule, fringe benefit changes, anticipated contract changes, price index (general cost changes), and known tax increases, should be made available to each department head from the accounting department. In addition, the historical information will be reviewed from prior plans and monthly reports on actual progress to date in the current year.

Any budget plan requires that certain forms and schedules be prepared for submission as a part of the formal budget. These are the summaries of worksheets that will be required in gathering detailed supporting material previously mentioned. These summaries and worksheets should be maintained for several years so that they can be referred to for answers to questions that may arise during the review stages and provide a recorded history of the reasoning behind certain decisions.

In addition to the required forms, each department head of the small hotel or motel should submit information describing in detail unusual items so that review questions and delays in approving the budget are kept at a minimum.

Consolidation of Departmental Plans

Upon completion, the departmental plans should be forwarded to the accounting department where they should be reviewed for clerical accuracy and completeness. The accounting department should be responsible for insuring that all forms and schedules are complete.

When the review is completed, the accounting department should prepare the Statement of Income for the entire property operation.

This statement, along with the detailed departmental statements and supporting data, would represent the total preliminary budget package for review by the general manager of the property. This preliminary budget should include any pertinent comments that arose during the accounting department's consolidation work.

Review by the General Manager and Preparation of Manager's Report

The property manager should review the summary Statement of Income and detail schedules to determine that all items are reasonable and that revenue and expense goals are realistic. During this review, particular attention must be directed to the coordination of all departments to insure that the operations plan for each department is fully recognized and reflected in the plans of the other departments.

Indicated earnings should be measured against the general manager's projection of the property's potential. Where additional adjustments are required, additional analysis of where and how the adjustments will be made must be made by the general manager in consultation with appropriate supervisory personnel. The potential effect on all departments of the property should be closely reviewed when a major change is made.

During the general manager's review of the plan, items for inclusion in the manager's report should be noted. These items plus the information arising from the budget planning meetings should provide the basic information for inclusion in the manager's report. The specific items to be contained in the manager's report should include a review of the following:

1. Competition
2. Economic conditions
3. Proposed changes in operations
4. Abnormal items
5. Personnel
6. Facilities
7. Rates
8. Capital improvements
9. Cash situation

When the general manager's review has been completed and his/her report drafted, a brief meeting should be held with the management personnel to go over the final budget.

The budget should then be submitted to the owners of the property for approval and adoption.

OPERATION OF THE BUDGET

Once the budget or forecast has been adopted, it must constantly be reviewed against actual results. This should be done often enough to be able to make adjustments and decisions to accommodate to changes in circumstances, business conditions, or newly disclosed facts.

Such comparisons normally should be made monthly, and variances between budgeted or forecasted and actual results should be analyzed to determine why such variances occurred so that corrective action, if required, can be taken quickly.

Generally, variances fall into the following categories:

1. Change in business conditions
2. Failure to control expenses
3. Errors

It is important to find the cause of the variance in order to determine the steps, if any, which need to be taken to correct the situation or to be able to accommodate new circumstances.

An example of the first category of variance would be where it is determined that prices of certain goods or services have increased more than expected. Alternate sources for such supplies may be considered, price increases may be deemed necessary, or a reduction in the amount of goods or services to be ordered might be appropriate. As another example, if convention blocks are not filling as planned, additional sales efforts can be instituted to make up for the indicated falloff for the balance of the year.

An example of the second type of variance would be the cost of an individual maid covering 10 rooms a shift rather than 15, as allowed under a union agreement, and/or the normal productivity for a single maid. Once this is determined the necessary corrective action can be instituted to increase the number of rooms serviced by the maid. Other examples would be placement of advertising in excess of planned amounts and failure to monitor utility billings in excess of expected usage.

Errors can be made in the budgeting or forecasting process or in recording expenditures. If relating to forecasting, a lesson has been learned which should result in improved budgeting or forecasting in the future. If relating to recording, correction is easy, and no substantive changes need be made other than those required if recording errors become a common occurrence.

If circumstances change materially, it may be necessary to prepare a new budget or forecast or, at a minimum, recognize that year-end results will be different than planned. This may then make it necessary to advise interested parties (such as owners) to expect different than budgeted or forecasted results.

FORMS OF STATEMENTS

The forms of the departmental statements used in this manual contain only one amount column, representing the figures for the period for which the statement is prepared. While the listing of revenue and expenses for the current period is the purpose in preparing a Statement of Income, the true significance of the amounts of revenue and expense can be understood only in their relation to each other, to plans prepared in advance (or budgets), and to the corresponding amounts of preceding periods. Statements of Income, therefore, should include such comparisons if they are to be meaningful. The preferred comparison is to a budget or forecast as this enables management to concentrate on decisions which will result in realization of pre-planned results. Comparisons to previous periods, although not as meaningful as comparisons to budgets, are a tool for property owners and managers to compare results with past performance as an indication of the success or failure of current performance. Comparisons should place emphasis on "variances" with an analysis explaining the variances in some detail.

The relation of expenses to revenue is expressed in terms of percentages. In each departmental statement of income, the basis of comparison — that is, the amount equivalent to 100% — should be the net sales of the department. Administrative and other unallocated expenses may be compared by means of percentages of the total sales and income from all sources. Percentages of all items may be given in separate columns of the various schedules, as shown in some of the illustrations given here; or the percentages of only the more important items of cost and expenses may be included at the bottom of the schedule or on a separate sheet.

The statement forms presented here illustrate a variety of comparative columnar arrangements. While these illustrations do not show all possible forms, they contain enough material for the preparation of a form suitable to any individual requirement.

In addition to indicating the percentage relation between revenue and expenses, the financial report of the small hotel or motel should contain sufficient statistical information to aid management in arriving at sound conclusions as to the efficiency of the operation of the various departments. The statistical information in the periodical reports is of even greater importance than the expense ratios, for the latter may be easily determined from the statements by simple calculations, while little of the essential statistical information can be thus obtained.

The following list indicates the kind of statistical information that the financial report of small hotels or motels should contain:

Rooms Department:
    Number of rooms in property
    Percentage of occupancy
    Percentage of double occupancy
    Average daily rate per occupied room
    Average house rate

Food and Beverage Department:
    Total food covers
    Average food check
    Combined food and beverage check
    Number of units (seats)
    Revenue per unit

Laundry Cost per 100 Pounds

Energy costs expressed in units of consumption:

Water	_____ cu. ft. or	_____ gal.
Electricity	_____ KWH	
Electrical demand	_____ KW	
Oil	_____ gal. type	_____
Coal	_____ tons	
Purchased steam	_____ lbs.	
Natural gas	_____ 100 cu. ft.	
L.P. gas	_____ lbs.	
Heating degree days	_____	
Cooling degree days	_____	

Salaries and Wages:
    Percentage to sales
    Percentage of employee benefits to total salaries and wages
    Percentage to sales — rooms department
    Percentage to sales — food and beverage department

General:
    Percentage or return on equity:
        Net earnings
        Cash flow (net earnings plus depreciation and amortization plus or
            minus net deferred income taxes and other items)
        Current ratio
        Debt — equity ratio

Such statistical information may be added to the respective departmental and expense schedules, or submitted in the form of a separate statistical schedule. (A brief discussion of selected ratios and an illustration of the computation of several of those ratios is presented on pages 95-98.)

SPECIMEN OF COLUMNAR FORMS

CURRENT MONTH			YEAR TO DATE		
Actual	Budget	Variance Increase (Decrease)	Actual	Budget	Variance Increase (Decrease)

CURRENT MONTH			YEAR TO DATE		
Actual	Budget	Last Year	Actual	Budget	Last Year

CURRENT MONTH			YEAR TO DATE		
Actual	Percentage	Last Year	Actual	Percentage	Last Year

CURRENT MONTH				YEAR TO DATE			
Actual	Percentage	Last Year	Percentage	Actual	Percentage	Last Year	Percentage

SPECIMEN OF COLUMNAR FORMS

		ACTUAL	BUDGET

		THIS YEAR	LAST YEAR

	ACTUAL	BUDGET	VARIANCE INCREASE [DECREASE]

	ACTUAL	BUDGET	LAST YEAR

CURRENT MONTH		YEAR TO DATE	
ACTUAL	BUDGET	ACTUAL	BUDGET

CURRENT MONTH		YEAR TO DATE	
THIS YEAR	LAST YEAR	THIS YEAR	LAST YEAR

Uniform Account Numbering System

The growing use of computers in the small hotel or motel industry has made more significant the uniform, orderly assignment of account numbers for compatibility with computer systems.

The numbering system should be first of all versatile. If a basic building-block system suitable for simple unit record equipment is used, it will also be suitable for more sophisticated equipment, and it can be more quickly committed to memory.

It should be broad enough to have a major number for each account that is to be used in standard reporting and sufficiently detailed to provide sub-accounts for all areas of significance in order to eliminate costly time-consuming account analysis.

The following example uses an eight-digit account numbering system:

XX — XXX — XXX

' ' ' — Sub-accounts

' ' — Major Accounts

' — Major Balance Sheet Classes
Revenue and Cost Centers

BALANCE SHEET CLASSES — MAJOR ACCOUNTS — SUB-ACCOUNTS

CURRENT ASSETS

Cash	*	**	***
House Bank #1	01	010	001
House Bank #2	01	010	002
House Bank #3	01	010	003
Demand Deposit ABC Bank	01	010	101
Demand Deposit XYZ Bank	01	010	102

* and ** on standard reporting under "Cash."
***Available for control and analysis

REVENUE AND COST CENTERS — MAJOR ACCOUNTS — SUB-ACCOUNTS

ROOMS

	*	**	***
Revenue — Trans. Reg.	51	001	000
Revenue — Trans. Group	51	002	000
Revenue — Perm.	51	003	000
Revenue — Extra Rm. Rev.	51	004	000
China, Glassware, Silver, Linen — China & Glass	51	110	001
China, Glassware, Silver, Linen — Silver	51	110	002
China, Glassware, Silver, Linen — Linen	51	110	003

* and ** on standard reporting.
***Available for control and analysis.

Ratio Analysis

Ratio analysis is the comparison of two or more figures resulting in a single, more meaningful figure. This ratio is then compared to a benchmark figure, which may be a budget figure, an industry average, or a past performance figure, to provide additional insight into the operation being analyzed. There are literally hundreds of ratios. A few which are most often used by industry personnel will be presented and grouped by the type of information desired. Both a short description and the formulation for each ratio will be provided. The Sample Motel used to illustrate the preparation of the Statement of Changes in Financial Position will be used to illustrate several ratios.

DESCRIPTION   FORMULATION

Liquidity Ratios — these ratios assist in the analysis of a small hotel or motel's ability to meet short-term obligations on a timely basis.

1. Current ratio — this ratio shows the relationship between a property's total current assets and total current liabilities.

$$\frac{\text{current assets}}{\text{current liabilities}}$$

2. Acid-test ratio — this ratio is a more stringent measure of liquidity as it reflects the relationship between a property's total quick assets and total current liabilities. Quick assets are generally considered to be the current assets of the property, less inventories and prepaid expenses.

$$\frac{\text{quick assets}}{\text{current liabilities}}$$

Solvency Ratios — these ratios assist in analyzing a small hotel or motel's ability to meet its long-term obligations on a timely basis.

1. Debt-equity ratio — this ratio expresses the total debt of the firm relative to the investment by the owners. Creditors view this ratio as an indicator of risk when credit extension relative to the small hotel or motel is considered.

$$\frac{\text{total debt}}{\text{total equity}}$$

DESCRIPTION	FORMULATION
2. Number of times interest earned — this ratio is another measure of risk as it indicates the number of times a firm could pay its interest expense.	$$\frac{\text{net income before income}}{\text{taxes + interest expense}}{\text{interest expense}}$$

Activity Ratios — these ratios assist in analyzing how effectively a small hotel or motel's assets are being used.

1. Average collection period — this ratio indicates the number of days required to collect the average accounts receivable.	$$\frac{\text{days in year}}{\text{total credit sales} \div}{\text{average accounts receivable}}$$
2. Inventory turnover — this ratio expresses the property's average amount of the inventory to the total cost of sales for the period. This ratio should be computed separately for food and beverage.	$$\frac{\text{cost of inventory used}}{\text{average inventory}}$$
3. Fixed assets turnover — this ratio indicates the revenues generated by fixed assets relative to these fixed assets. Since fixed assets are generally the major portion of assets of a property, it is a reasonable measure for evaluating the utilization of assets.	$$\frac{\text{total revenues generated by fixed assets}}{\text{average total fixed assets}}$$
4. Percentage of occupancy — this ratio is a measure of the total rooms sold to total rooms available for a small hotel or motel.	$$\frac{\text{total rooms sold}}{\text{total rooms available}}$$
5. Percentage of double occupancy — this ratio shows what percentage of rooms sold contain more than one guest.	$$\frac{\text{total rooms sold with multiple occupancy}}{\text{total rooms sold}}$$

Profitability Ratios — these ratios assist in analyzing profitability of the firm.

1. Return on owners' equity — this ratio shows the relationship between net income and average owners' equity.	$$\frac{\text{net income}}{\text{average owners' equity}}$$
2. Return on assets — this ratio reflects the relationship between net income and average total assets.	$$\frac{\text{net income}}{\text{average total assets}}$$

3. Profit margin — this ratio indicates the net income of the property as a percentage of total revenue. This percentage, when multiplied by $1, shows the amount of net income per each dollar of revenue.

$$\frac{\text{net income}}{\text{total revenue}}$$

Operating Ratios — these ratios assist in analyzing the operations of a property.

1. Average room rate — this ratio shows the average rate charged per room sold.

$$\frac{\text{total room revenues}}{\text{number of rooms sold}}$$

2. Average restaurant check — this ratio indicates the average amount charged per cover. This may be calculated separately for food and beverage.

$$\frac{\text{total restaurant sales}}{\text{number of covers}}$$

3. Food cost percentage — this ratio shows the cost of food sold as a percentage of total food sales.

$$\frac{\text{cost of food sold}}{\text{total food sales}}$$

4. Beverage cost percentage — this ratio expresses the cost of beverages sold as a percentage of total beverage sales.

$$\frac{\text{cost of beverages sold}}{\text{total beverage sales}}$$

RATIO ANALYSIS ILLUSTRATED

The Sample Motel's Financial information, presented on pages 76 and 77, is used to illustrate several of the preceding ratios.

		Beginning of Year	End of Year
1. Current ratio =	$\dfrac{\text{current assets}}{\text{current liabilities}}$	$\dfrac{19,000}{9,000}$ = 2.1 to 1	$\dfrac{20,000}{8,000}$ = 2.5 to 1
2. Acid-test ratio =	$\dfrac{\text{quick assets}}{\text{current liabilities}}$	$\dfrac{15,000}{9,000}$ = 1.7 to 1	$\dfrac{16,500}{8,000}$ = 2.1 to 1
3. Debt-equity ratio =	$\dfrac{\text{total liabilities}}{\text{total owners' equity}}$	$\dfrac{109,000}{70,000}$ = 1.56 to 1	$\dfrac{110,000}{76,000}$ = 1.45 to 1

		Ratio for Period
4. Number of times interest earned =	$\dfrac{\text{net income before income taxes + interest expense}}{\text{interest expense}}$	$\dfrac{15,000}{5,000}$ = 3 times
5. Average collection period =	$\dfrac{\text{days in year}}{\text{total credit sales} \div \text{average accounts receivable}}$	$\dfrac{365}{*180,000 \div ** 11,000}$ = 22.3 days
6. Fixed asset turnover =	$\dfrac{\text{total revenues generated by fixed assets}}{\text{average total fixed assets}}$	$\dfrac{180,000}{163,000}$ = 1.1 times
7. Return on owners' equity =	$\dfrac{\text{net income}}{\text{average owners' equity}}$	$\dfrac{7,000}{73,000}$ = 9.6%
8. Return on assets =	$\dfrac{\text{net income}}{\text{average total assets}}$	$\dfrac{7,000}{182,500}$ = 3.84%
9. Profit margin =	$\dfrac{\text{net income}}{\text{total revenue}}$	$\dfrac{7,000}{180,000}$ = 3.9%
10. Food inventory turnover =	$\dfrac{\text{cost of inventory used}}{\text{average food inventory}}$	$\dfrac{20,000}{2,000}$ = 10 times
11. Average room rate =	$\dfrac{\text{total room sales}}{\text{number of rooms sold}}$	$\dfrac{120,000}{6,000}$ = $20
12. Average restaurant check =	$\dfrac{\text{total food sales}}{\text{number of covers}}$	$\dfrac{50,000}{12,000}$ = $4.17
13. Food cost percentage =	$\dfrac{\text{cost of food sold}}{\text{food sales}}$	$\dfrac{20,000}{50,000}$ = 40%

*Assumes total revenue is total credit sales
**The beginning and ending accounts receivable divided by two.

Expense Dictionary

This dictionary has been compiled to serve the Uniform System of Accounts for Small Hotels and Motels. It will be noted that it has been designed to cover properties with and without restaurant operations. Accordingly, it will be necessary to refer to the proper column when looking up the account classification that applies to a particular item.

ABBREVIATIONS

Departmental names which appear frequently and are rather lengthy have been shortened as follows:

DEPARTMENT	ABBREVIATION
Administrative and General	A&G
Depreciation and Amortization	Depr. & Amort.
Food and Beverages	F&B
Property Operation, Maintenance and Energy Costs	POM&E
Rent, Property Taxes and Other Municipal Charges and Insurance	Rent, Property Taxes, etc.
Other abbreviations include:	
Advertising	Adv.
Electrical & Mechanical Equipment	Elec. & Mech. Equip.
Printing, Stationery & Postage	Prtg., Stat. & Post.
Marketing	Mktg.

Expense Dictionary

Items	No Restaurant Operation	Restaurant Operation

A

Abrasive Files	POM&E—Operating Supplies & Misc.	POM&E—Operating Supplies
Absorbent Cotton	Employee Benefits	Employee Benefits—Misc.
Accountants' Fees— Beverage Cost		F&B—Other Operating Expenses
Accountants' Fees— Food Cost		F&B—Other Operating Expenses
Accountants' Fees— Public Accountants	General—Professional Fees	A&G—Professional Fees
Acids—Cleaning	Rooms—Operating Supplies	Rooms; F&B—Operating Supplies
Acids—Laundry		House Laundry—Laundry Supplies
Adding Machine—Service	POM&E—R&M	POM&E—Elec. & Mech. Equip.
Adding Machine—Tapes	General—Prtg., Stat. & Post.	F&B—Operating Supplies; A&G—Prtg. & Stat.
Addressing Envelopes & Cards	General—Mktg.	Mktg.—Other Selling & Promotional Expenses
Addressing Machine Plates	General—Mktg.	Mktg.—Other Selling & Promotional Expenses
Addressing Machine Stencils	General—Mktg.	Mktg.—Other Selling & Promotional Expenses
Adhesive Tape	POM&E—Operating Supplies & Misc.	POM&E—Misc.
Adhesive Tape	Employee Benefits	Employee Benefits—Misc.

Items	No Restaurant Operation	Restaurant Operation
Advertising Agency Fees	General—Mktg.	Mktg.—Fees & Commissions —Agency Fees
Advertising—Buses	General—Mktg.	Mktg.—Adv.—Outdoor
Advertising—Due Bills for Room, etc.	General—Mkgt.	Mktg.—Adv.—Other Adv. Expenses
Advertising—Foreign Publications	General—Mktg.	Mktg.—Adv.—Print
Advertising—Guide Books ..	General—Mktg.	Mktg.—Adv.—Print
Advertising—Journals	General—Mktg.	Mktg.—Adv.—Print
Advertising—Labels	General—Mktg.	Mktg.—Adv.—Other Adv. Expenses
Advertising—Magazines	General—Mktg.	Mktg.—Adv.—Print
Advertising—Newspapers ...	General—Mktg.	Mktg.—Adv.—Print
Advertising—Novelties	General—Mktg.	Mktg.—Adv.—Other Adv. Expenses
Advertising—Outdoor	General—Mktg.	Mktg.—Adv.—Outdoor
Advertising—Periodicals	General—Mktg.	Mktg.—Adv.—Print
Advertising—Radios	General—Mktg.	Mktg.—Adv.—Radio & TV
Advertising—Railroad Trains	General—Mktg.	Mktg.—Adv.—Outdoor
Advertising—Subways	General—Mktg.	Mktg.—Adv.—Outdoor
Advertising—Taxicabs	General—Mktg.	Mktg.—Adv.—Outdoor
Advertising—Telephone Directories	General—Mktg.	Mktg.—Adv.—Print
Advertising—Television	General—Mktg.	Mktg.—Adv.—Radio & TV
Advertising—Theatre Programs	General—Mktg.	Mktg.—Adv.—Print
Air-Cooling Systems Repairs	POM&E—R&M	POM&E—Elec. & Mech. Equip.
Air Mail Stickers	Rooms—Operating Supplies .	Rooms—Operating Supplies
Airport Transportation—Not Chargeable to Guest	General—A&G; Mktg.	A&G—Traveling Expenses; Mktg. —Other Selling & Promotional Expenses
Alarm Service—Fire or Burglar	General—Security	A&G—Security
Alcohol—Cleaning	Rooms—Operating Supplies .	Rooms; F&B—Operating Supplies
Alcohol—Cooking Fuel		F&B—Kitchen Fuel
Alcohol—Painting	POM&E—R&M	POM&E—Furniture, Fixtures, Equipment & Decor
Alkalies (Water Softeners) ...	POM&E—Operating Supplies & Misc.	POM&E—Engineering Supplies
Aluminum Trays		F&B—Other Operating Expenses
Ammeter Repairs	POM&E—R&M	POM&E—Elec. & Mech. Equip.
Ammonia—Cleaning	Rooms—Operating Supplies .	Rooms; F&B—Operating Supplies
Ammonia—Refrigerant	POM&E—Operating Supplies & Misc.	POM&E—Elec. & Mech. Equip.
Ammonia Water—Cleaning ..	Rooms—Operating Supplies .	Rooms; F&B—Operating Supplies
Ammonia Water—Laundering		House Laundry—Laundry Supplies
Amortization—Bond Discount	Fixed Charges— Interest Expense	Interest Expense—Amort. of Deferred Finance Costs
Amortization—Bond Expense	Fixed Charges— Interest Expense	Interest Expense—Amort. of Deferred Finance Costs

Items	_No Restaurant Operation_	_Restaurant Operation_
Amortization—Financing Costs	Fixed Charges— Interest Expense	Interest Expense—Amort. of Deferred Finance Costs
Amortization—Mort. Expense	Fixed Charges— Interest Expense	Interest Expense—Amort. of Deferred Finance Costs
Amortization—Leasehold ...	Fixed Charges— Interest Expense	Depr. & Amort.—Amort.— Leaseholds & Improvements
Amortization—Leasehold Improvements	Fixed Charges— Depr. & Amort.	Depr. & Amort.—Amort.— Leasehold & Improvements
Analyses—Chemical	POM&E—Operating Supplies & Misc.	F&B—Other Operating Expenses
Angle Iron	POM&E—R&M	POM&E—Building
Announcements		F&B—Operating Supplies
Announcements—Advertising	General—Mktg.	Mktg.—Adv.—Other Adv. Expenses
Announcement Cards on Tables		F&B—Operating Supplies
Appetizers—Bar		F&B—Other Operating Expenses
Aprons	Rooms—Uniforms	Rooms; F&B; House Laundry —Uniforms
Aprons for Mangles		House Laundry—Laundry Supplies
Aquariums	Rooms—Misc.	Rooms; F&B—Other Operating Expenses
Armored Car Service	General—Security	A&G—Security
Art Work	General—Mktg.	Mktg.—Merchandising
Artificial Flowers	Rooms—Misc.	Rooms; F&B—Other Operating Expenses
Arts & Crafts Supplies	Rooms—Misc.	Rooms; F&B—Other Operating Expenses
Asbestos Pipe Covering	POM&E—R&M	POM&E—Elec. & Mech. Equip.
Ash Cans	POM&E—Operating Supplies & Misc.	POM&E—Removal of Waste Matter
Ash Trays—China & Glass ..	Rooms—China, Glassware & Linen	Rooms—China, Glassware & Linen; F&B—China, Glass, Silver & Linen
Ashes—Removal of	POM&E—Operating Supplies & Misc.	POM&E—Removal of Waste Matter
Asphalt	POM&E—R&M	POM&E—Building
Association Dues—Marketing Employees	General Mktg.	Mktg.—Other Selling and Promotional Expenses
Association Dues—Other Than Mktg. Employees ...	General—Trade Assn. Dues & Trade Publications	A&G—Trade Assn. Dues & Trade Publications
Athletic Equipment for Employees	Employee Benefits	Employee Benefits—Other Expenses—Misc.
Atomizing—Cups	POM&E—R&M	POM&E—Elec. & Mech. Equip.

Items	No Restaurant Operation	Restaurant Operation
Attorneys' Fees—For Collections	General—Misc.	A&G—Misc.
Attorneys' Fees—Other Than Collections	General—Professional Fees	A&G—Professional Fees
Audit Fees—Public Accountants	General—Professional Fees	A&G—Professional Fees
Augers	POM&E—Operating Supplies & Misc.	POM&E—Operating Supplies
Auto Hire	Rooms—Misc.	Rooms; F&B; etc.—Other Operating Expenses
Auto Rental	General—A&G; Mktg.	A&G—Traveling Expenses, Mktg.—Other Selling & Promotional Expenses
Auto Supplies	Cost of Gas, Oil, Auto Supplies Purchased	Garage; etc.—Cost of Sales
Auto—Truck Repairs	POM&E—R&M	POM&E—Elec. & Mech. Equip.
Automatic Shutters	POM&E—R&M	POM&E—Elec. & Mech. Equip.
Automatic Telephone Rentals	General—Misc.	A&G—Misc.
Awards for Suggestions by Employees	Employee Benefits	Employee Benefits—Other Expenses—Misc.
Awning—Cleaning	Rooms—Laundry & Dry Cleaning	Rooms; F&B—Laundry & Dry Cleaning
Awning Repairs	POM&E—R&M	POM&E—Misc.
Axes—Fire	General—Misc.	A&G—Misc.

B

Items	No Restaurant Operation	Restaurant Operation
Bad Debts	General—Misc.	A&G—Provision for Doubtful Accounts
Badges	Rooms—Uniforms	Rooms; F&B; etc.—Uniforms
Baggage Checks	Rooms—Operating Supplies	Rooms—Operating Supplies
Baggage Labels	Rooms—Operating Supplies	Rooms—Operating Supplies
Baggage Tags	Rooms—Operating Supplies	Rooms—Operating Supplies
Baggage Transfer—Outside Companies	Rooms—Misc.	Rooms—Other Operating Expenses
Bags (Laundry)		House Laundry—Laundry Supplies
Bain Marie		F&B—Other Operating Expenses
Ball Bearings	POM&E—R&M	POM&E—Elec. & Mech. Equip.
Band Saws	POM&E—R&M	POM&E—Elec. & Mech. Equip.
Bank Checks	General—Prtg., Stat. & Post.	A&G—Prtg. & Stat.
Bank Exchange on Checks & Currency	General—Misc.	A&G—Misc.
Banners	Rooms—Misc.	Rooms; F&B—Other Operating Expenses
Banquet Expenses		F&B—Other Operating Expenses
Banquet Reports		F&B—Other Operating Expenses
Banquet Set-up Blueprints		Mktg.—Merchandising
Bar Appetizers		F&B—Other Operating Expenses
Bar Expenses		F&B—Other Operating Expenses
Bar Supplies		F&B—Other Operating Expenses

Items	No Restaurant Operation	Restaurant Operation
Bar Utensils		F&B—Other Operating Expenses
Barrel—Silver, Repairs		POM&E—Elec. & Mech. Equip.
Basket Liners, Waste Paper .	Rooms—Operating Supplies .	Rooms; F&B—Operating Supplies
Bath Mats	Rooms—China, Glassware & Linen	Rooms—China, Glassware & Linen
Bathroom Glass Shelves	POM&E—R&M	POM&E—Building
Bathing Caps (Guest)	Rooms—Operating Supplies .	Rooms—Operating Supplies
Batter Bowls		F&B—Other Operating Expenses
Batter Mixers		F&B—Other Operating Expenses
Batteries & Flashlights	POM&E—Operating Supplies & Misc.	POM&E—Operating Supplies
Beaters		F&B—Other Operating Expenses
Bed Pads	Rooms—China, Glassware & Linen	Rooms—China, Glassware & Linen
Bed Springs	POM&E—R&M	POM&E—Furniture, Fixtures, Equip. & Decor
Bedspreads	Rooms—China, Glassware & Linen	Rooms—China, Glassware & Linen
Bedspreads—Cleaning	Rooms—Laundry & Dry Cleaning	Rooms—Laundry & Dry Cleaning
Beer Coils		F&B—Other Operating Expenses
Beer Foam Scrapers		F&B—Other Operating Expenses
Belts—Canvas	POM&E—R&M	POM&E—Elec. & Mech. Equip.
Belts—Window Cleaners	Rooms—Operating Supplies .	Rooms; F&B—Operating Supplies
Belts—Leather	POM&E—R&M	POM&E—Elec. & Mech. Equip.
Belts—Rubber	POM&E—R&M	POM&E—Elec. & Mech. Equip.
Benzine	POM&E—R&M	POM&E—Furniture, Fixtures, Equip. & Decor
Benzine—Cleaning	Rooms—Operating Supplies .	Rooms; F&B—Operating Supplies
Beverage Licenses		F&B—Licenses
Beverage Lists		F&B—Operating Supplies
Beverage Mixers		F&B—Other Operating Expenses
Beverage Signs		F&B—Other Operating Expenses
Beverage Spoons		F&B—Other Operating Expenses
Beverage Stirrers—Glass		F&B—Other Operating Expenses
Beverage Taxes		F&B—Cost of Beverages Sold
Billboards	General—Mktg.	Mktg.—Adv.—Outdoor
Billing Machine Supplies	General—Prtg., Stat. & Post.	A&G—Prtg. & Stat.
Bills of Fare		F&B—Operating Supplies
Bin Cards—Liquor		F&B—Operating Supplies

Items	No Restaurant Operation	Restaurant Operation
Binders	General—Prtg., Stat. & Post.	A&G—Prtg. & Stat.; Rooms; F&B: etc.—Operating Supplies
Birds (& Bird Seed)	Rooms—Misc.	Rooms—Other Operating Expenses; F&B—Operating Supplies
Blades—Razor (Guest)	Rooms—Operating Supplies	Rooms—Operating Supplies
Blankets	Rooms—China, Glassware & Linen	Rooms—China, Glassware & Linen
Blankets—Cleaning	Rooms—Laundry & Dry Cleaning	Rooms—Laundry & Dry Cleaning
Bleach		House Laundry—Laundry Supplies
Blinds	POM&E—R&M	POM&E—Furniture, Fixtures, Equip. & Decor
Blinds—Venetian	POM&E—R&M	POM&E—Furniture, Fixtures, Equip. & Decor
Blotters—Advertising	General—Mktg.	Mktg.—Merchandising
Blotters (Employees)	Rooms—Operating Supplies; Gen.—Prtg., Stat. & Post.	Rooms; F&B—Other Operating Expenses; A&G—Prtg. & Stat.
Blotters (Guest)	Rooms—Operating Supplies	Rooms—Operating Supplies
Blouses	Rooms—Uniforms	Rooms; F&B; House Laundry—Uniforms
Blueprints—Banquet Set-up		Mktg.—Merchandising
Bluing		House Laundry—Laundry Supplies
Boiler Compound	POM&E—Operating Supplies & Misc.	POM&E—Engineering Supplies
Boiler Explosion Insurance	Fixed Charges—Insurance	Rent, Property, Taxes, etc.—Insurance on Bldg. & Contents
Boiler Gauges	POM&E—R&M	POM&E—Elec. & Mech. Equip.
Boiler Inspection	POM&E—R&M	POM&E—Elec. & Mech. Equip.
Boiler Repairs	POM&E—R&M	POM&E—Elec. & Mech. Equip.
Bond Discount	Interest Expense	Interest Expense—Amort. of Deferred Financing Costs
Bond Expense Amortization	Fixed Charges—Interest Expense	Interest Expense—Amort. of Deferred Financing Costs
Bond Interest	Fixed Charges—Interest Expense	Interest Expense—Other Long-Term Debt
Bonds—Fidelity	General—Insurance	A&G—Insurance—General
Bonuses—Employees	Employee Benefits	Rooms; F&B; etc.—Employee Benefits
Booklets—Advertising	General—Mktg.	Mktg.—Merchandising
Book Matches (Guest)	Rooms—Operating Supplies	Rooms; F&B—Operating Supplies
Books—Account	General—Prtg., Stat. & Post.	A&G—Prtg. & Stat.
Books—for Employees' Use	Employee Benefits	Employee Benefits—Misc.
Books—Guest Library	Rooms—Misc.	Rooms—Other Operating Expenses
Books, Log	Rooms—Operating Supplies	Rooms; F&B; etc.—Operating Supplies

Items	No Restaurant Operation	Restaurant Operation
Books—Records	General—Prtg., Stat. & Post.	Rooms; F&B—Operating Supplies; A&G—Prtg. & Stat.
Books—Technical	General—Trade Assn. Dues & Trade Publications	A&G—Trade Assn. Dues & Trade Publications
Booths—Trade Shows	General—Mktg.	Mktg.—Sales—Other Selling Expenses
Boots	Rooms—Uniforms	Rooms; F&B—Uniforms
Boots—Leather	Rooms—Uniforms	Rooms; F&B—Uniforms
Boots—Rubber	Rooms—Uniforms	Rooms; F&B—Uniforms
Bottle Openers		F&B—Other Operating Expenses
Bottle Openers (Guest)	Rooms—Operating Supplies	Rooms—Operating Supplies
Boutonnieres (Employees)	Rooms—Uniforms	Rooms; F&B—Uniforms
Boutonnieres (Guest)	Rooms—Operating Supplies	F&B—Operating Supplies
Bowls—Batter		F&B—Other Operating Expenses
Bowls—China		F&B—China, Glass, Silver & Linen
Bowls—Glass		F&B—China, Glass, Silver & Linen
Bowls—Mixing		F&B—Other Operating Expenses
Bowls—Salad		F&B—China, Glass, Silver & Linen
Boxes—Laundry		House Laundry—Laundry Supplies
Boxes—Pastry		F&B—Operating Supplies
Braid for Uniforms	Rooms—Uniforms	Rooms; F&B—Uniforms
Brass Polish	Rooms—Operating Supplies	Rooms; F&B—Operating Supplies
Bread & Butter Plates		F&B—China, Glass, Silver & Linen
Breakdown Service—Electric	POM&E—R&M	POM&E—Elec. & Mech. Equip.
Bricks—Fire	POM&E—R&M	POM&E—Elec. & Mech. Equip.
Bridge Place Cards (Guest)	Rooms—Operating Supplies	Rooms; F&B—Operating Supplies
Bridge Prizes (Guest)	Rooms—Operating Supplies	Rooms; F&B—Operating Supplies
Bridge Score Pads (Guest)	Rooms—Operating Supplies	Rooms; F&B—Operating Supplies
Brine	POM&E—R&M	POM&E—Elec. & Mech. Equip.
Briquets		F&B—Kitchen Fuel
Broadcasting	General—Mktg.	Mktg.—Adv.—Radio & TV
Brochette Needles		F&B—Other Operating Expenses
Brochures	General—Mktg.	Mktg.—Merchandising
Brooms	Rooms—Operating Supplies	Rooms; F&B—Operating Supplies
Brushes—Cleaning	Rooms—Operating Supplies	Rooms; F&B—Operating Supplies
Brushes—Dust	Rooms—Operating Supplies	Rooms; F&B—Operating Supplies
Brushes—Generator	POM&E—R&M	POM&E—Elec. & Mech. Equip.
Brushes (Guest)	Rooms—Operating Supplies	Rooms—Operating Supplies

Items	No Restaurant Operation	Restaurant Operation
Brushes—Paint	POM&E—R&M	POM&E—Furniture, Fixtures, Equip. & Decor
Buffing Compound	Rooms—Operating Supplies	Rooms; F&B—Operating Supplies
Building & Contents Insurance	Fixed Charges—Insurance	Rent, Property Taxes, etc.—Insurance on Bldg. & Contents
Building Depreciation	Fixed Charges—Depr.	Depr. & Amort.—Depr.—Bldg. & Improvements Improvements
Building Insurance	Fixed Charges—Insurance	Rent, Property Taxes, etc.—Insurance on Bldg. & Contents
Building Repairs	POM&E—R&M	POM&E—Building
Building Repairs—Outside Contract	POM&E—R&M	POM&E—Building
Bulletin Board Supplies	Rooms—Misc.	Rooms—Other Operating Expenses
Bunting & Flags	Rooms—Misc.	Rooms; F&B—Other Operating Expenses
Burglar Alarm Service	General—Security	A&G—Security
Burglary Insurance	General—Insurance—General	A&G—Insurance—General
Burlap	POM&E—R&M	POM&E—Furniture, Fixtures, Equip. & Decor
Bus Advertising	General—Mktg.	Mktg.—Adv.—Outdoor
Business Cards	General—Prtg., Stat. & Post.	Rooms; F&B; etc.—Operating Supplies
Business Promotion Traveling Expenses	General—Mktg.	Mktg.—Sales—Other Selling Expenses
Butter Chips (Paper)		F&B—Operating Supplies
Butter Chips (Silver)		F&B—China, Glass, Silver & Linen
Button Hooks	Rooms—Operating Supplies	Rooms—Operating Supplies
Buttons (Guest)	Rooms—Operating Supplies	Rooms—Operating Supplies
Buttons—Laundry		House Laundry—Laundry Supplies
Buttons—Uniforms	Rooms—Uniforms	Rooms; F&B; etc.—Uniforms

C

Items	No Restaurant Operation	Restaurant Operation
Cablegrams	General—Telephone & Telegrams	A&G—Postage & Telegrams
Cables—Elevator	POM&E—R&M	POM&E—Elec. & Mech. Equip.
Calcium	POM&E—Operating Supplies & Misc.	POM&E—Engineering Supplies
Calculating Machines—Maintenance	POM&E—R&M	POM&E—Elec. & Mech. Equip.
Calendars	General—Mktg.	Mktg.—Merchandising
Can Openers		F&B—Other Operating Expenses
Candles	Rooms—China, Glassware & Linen	Rooms—China, Glassware & Linen; F&B—China, Glass, Silver & Linen

108

Items	No Restaurant Operation	Restaurant Operation
Candlesticks—China	Rooms—China, Glassware & Linen	Rooms—China, Glassware & Linen; F&B—China, Glass, Silver & Linen
Candy (Guest)	Rooms—Operating Supplies	Rooms; F&B—Operating Supplies
Canvas—Painting	POM&E—R&M	POM&E—Furniture, Fixtures, Equip. & Decor
Caps	Rooms—Uniforms	Rooms; F&B—Uniforms
Caps—Bathing (Guest)	Rooms—Operating Supplies	Rooms—Operating Supplies
Car Cards	General—Mktg.	Mktg.—Adv.—Outdoor
Carafes	Rooms—China, Glassware & Linen	Rooms—China, Glassware & Linen; F&B—China, Glass, Silver & Linen
Carbon Paper	General—Prtg., Stat. & Post	Rooms; F&B—Operating Supplies; A&G—Prtg. & Stationery
Carbonated Gas		F&B—Cost of Beverage Sales
Card Addressing	General—Mktg.	Mktg.—Other Selling & Promotional Expenses
Cardboard Boxes		F&B—Operating Supplies
Cardboard — Laundry		House Laundry—Laundry Supplies
Carfares	General—Misc.	A&G—Misc.
Carpet Linings	POM&E—R&M	POM&E—Furniture, Fixtures, Equip. & Decor
Carpet Repairs	POM&E—R&M	POM&E—Furniture, Fixtures, Equip. & Decor
Carpet & Rugs—Cleaning	Rooms—Laundry & Dry Cleaning	Rooms—Laundry & Dry Cleaning
Carpet Sweepers	Rooms—Operating Supplies	Rooms; F&B—Operating Supplies
Carpet Tacks	POM&E—R&M	POM&E—Furniture, Fixtures, Equip. & Decor
Carpet Washer	Rooms—Operating Supplies	Rooms; F&B—Operating Supplies
Cash Overage & Shortage	General—Misc.	A&G—Misc.
Cash Register—Repairs	POM&E—R&M	POM&E—Elec. & Mech. Equip.
Cash Register Supplies	Rooms—Operating Supplies	Rooms; F&B—Operating Supplies
Cash Reports	General—Prtg., Stat. & Post.	A&G—Prtg. & Stat.
Cashier Sheets	General—Prtg., Stat. & Post.	A&G—Prtg. & Stat.
Casseroles		F&B—China, Glass, Silver & Linen
Caustic Soda	Rooms—Operating Supplies	Rooms; F&B—Operating Supplies
Ceiling Repairs	POM&E—R&M	POM&E—Building
Cellophane		F&B—Operating Supplies
Cement, Adhesive	POM&E—R&M	POM&E—Building
Cement, Asphalt	POM&E—R&M	POM&E—Building
Chair Rentals—Banquets		F&B—Other Operating Expenses
Non-Banquets	Rooms—Misc.	Rooms—Other Operating Expenses
Chalk	Rooms—Misc.	Rooms; F&B—Other Operating Expenses

Items	No Restaurant Operation	Restaurant Operation
Chamois	Rooms—Operating Supplies	Rooms; F&B—Operating Supplies
Charcoal		F&B—Kitchen Fuel
Charge Vouchers	Rooms—Operating Supplies	Rooms; F&B—Operating Supplies
Charts—Meter	POM&E—Operating Supplies & Misc.	POM&E—Operating Supplies
Checking Supplies		F&B—Operating Supplies
Checks—Bank	General—Prtg., Stat. & Post.	A&G—Prtg. & Stat.
Checks—Restaurant		F&B—Operating Supplies
Checks—Waiter		F&B—Operating Supplies
Cheesecloth	Rooms—Operating Supplies; POM&E—R&M	Rooms—Operating Supplies; POM&E—Furniture, Fixtures, Equip. & Decor
Cheesecloth (for Straining)		F&B—Other Operating Expenses
Chemicals—Fire Extinguisher	General—Misc.	A&G—Misc.
Chemicals—Laundry		House Laundry—Laundry Supplies
Chemicals (Mothproofing of Carpets)	Rooms—Operating Supplies	Rooms; F&B—Operating Supplies
Chemicals (Water Treatment)	Swimming Pool Expense	POM&E—Engineering Supplies
China	Rooms—China, Glassware & Linen	Rooms—China, Glassware & Linen
China Bowls		F&B—China, Glass, Silver & Linen
China Cups		F&B—China, Glass, Silver & Linen
China Dishes		F&B—China, Glass, Silver & Linen
China Pitchers	Rooms—China, Glassware & Linen	Rooms—China, Glassware & Linen; F&B—China, Glass, Silver & Linen
China Platters		F&B—China, Glass, Silver & Linen
China Trays	Rooms—China, Glassware & Linen	Rooms—China, Glassware & Linen; F&B—China, Glass, Silver & Linen
Chintz	POM&E—R&M	POM&E—Furniture, Fixtures, Equip. & Decor
Chloride of Lime		House Laundry—Laundry Supplies
Chlorine	Swimming Pool Expense	POM&E—Engineering Supplies
Chop Frills		F&B—Operating Supplies
Chop Holders		F&B—Operating Supplies
Christmas Expense	General—Misc.	A&G—Misc.
Christmas Presents & Gratuities (Other Than Employees)	General—Misc.	A&G—Misc.
Christmas Trees & Decorations	General—Misc.	Rooms; F&B—Other Operating Expenses
Cigarettes (Guest)	Rooms—Operating Supplies	F&B—Operating Supplies
Cigars (Guest)	Rooms—Operating Supplies	F&B—Operating Supplies
Circulars	General—Mktg.	Mktg.—Merchandising

Items	No Restaurant Operation	Restaurant Operation
Civic & Community Projects .	General—Mktg.	Mktg.—Public Relations & Publicity
Cleaning Bedspreads	Rooms—Laundry & Dry Cleaning	Rooms—Laundry & Dry Cleaning
Cleaning Beer Coils		F&B—Other Operating Expenses
Cleaning Compounds	Rooms—Operating Supplies .	Rooms; F&B—Operating Supplies
Cleaning Dining Rooms (On Contract)		F&B—Contract Cleaning
Cleaning Fluids	Rooms—Operating Supplies .	Rooms; F&B—Operating Supplies
Cleaning Pantries		F&B—Contract Cleaning
Cleaning Rags	Rooms—Operating Supplies .	Rooms; F&B—Operating Supplies
Cleaning Streets	General—Misc.	A&G—Misc.
Cleaning Supplies	Rooms—Operating Supplies .	Rooms; F&B; etc.— Operating Supplies
Cleaning Supplies—Food ...	Cost of Food Purchased & Incidental Expenses	F&B—Operating Supplies
Clinic—Employees	Employee Benefits	Employee Benefits—Misc.
Clippings	General—Mktg.	Mktg.—Adv.—Other Adv. Expenses
Clips	General—Prtg., Stat. & Post.	Rooms; F&B—Operating Supplies; A&G; House Laundry—Prtg. & Stat.
Clothes Hangers (Guest)	Rooms—Operating Supplies .	Rooms—Operating Supplies
Clothing Repairs—Outside Establishments	Rooms—Uniforms	Rooms; F&B—Uniforms
Clothing Reweaving (Guest) .	General—Misc.	A&G—Misc.
Coal—Cooking		F&B—Kitchen Fuel
Coal—Heating	POM&E—Fuel	POM&E—Fuel
Coal Shovels	POM&E—Operating Supplies & Misc.	POM&E—Engineering Supplies
Coat Hangers (Guest)	Rooms—Operating Supplies .	Rooms—Operating Supplies
Coats	Rooms—Uniforms	Rooms; F&B—Uniforms
Coats, Rubber—for Doormen	Rooms—Uniforms	Rooms—Uniforms
Cocktail Napkins—Paper ...		F&B—Operating Supplies
Cocktail Shakers		F&B—Other Operating Expenses
Coffee (Free)	Rooms—Operating Supplies .	Rooms—Operating Supplies
Coffec Bags		F&B—Other Operating Expenses
Coffee Pots—China		F&B—China, Glass, Silver & Linen
Coffee Pots—Glass		F&B—China, Glass, Silver & Linen
Coffee Pots—Silver		F&B—China, Glass, Silver & Linen
Coffee Urn Repairs		POM&E—Elec. & Mech. Equip.
Coin Bags	General—Misc.	A&G—Misc.
Coin Wrappers	General—Misc.	A&G—Misc.
Colanders		Food—Other Operating Expenses
Collars	Rooms—Uniforms	Rooms; F&B—Uniforms
Collecting Guest Accounts ..	General—Misc.	A&G—Misc.
Collection Expense	General—Misc.	A&G—Misc.
Collection Fees—Attorneys .	General—Misc.	A&G—Misc.

Items	No Restaurant Operation	Restaurant Operation
Colored Spreads	Rooms—China, Glassware & Linen	Rooms—China, Glassware & Linen
Combs—Guest	Rooms—Operating Supplies	Rooms—Operating Supplies
Commissions—Beverage		F&B—Salaries & Wages
Commissions—Credit Card Charge	General—Misc.	A&G—Commission on Credit Card Charges—Net
Commissions—Food		F&B—Salaries & Wages
Commissions—F&B		F&B—Salaries & Wages
Commissions—F&B (Non-Employees)		F&B—Other Operating Expenses
Commissions—Rental Agents	Rooms—Commissions	Rooms—Commissions
Commissions—Tour Agencies	Rooms—Commissions	Rooms—Commissions
Communicating System—Internal	General—Misc.	A&G—Misc.
Complimentary Beverage		Mktg.—Other Selling & Promotion Expense
Complimentary Beverage—Musicians & Entertainers		F&B—Music & Entertainment
Complimentary Entertaining at Motel	General—Mktg.	Mktg.—Other Selling & Promotion Expenses
Complimentary Food		Mktg.—Other Selling & Promotion Expenses
Complimentary Food—Musicians & Entertainers		F&B—Music & Entertainment
Complimentary Parking	Rooms—Misc.	Rooms; F&B; etc.—Other Operating Expenses
Complimentary Rooms	General—Mktg.	Mktg.—Other Selling & Promotion Expenses
Complimentary Rooms—Musicians & Entertainers		F&B—Music & Entertainment
Composition	General—Mktg.	Mktg.—Adv.—Other Adv. Expenses
Compotes		F&B—China, Glass, Silver & Linen
Consultant Fees, Professional	General—Professional Fees	A&G—Professional Fees
Containers—Liquid, Paper		F&B—Operating Supplies
Contents Insurance	Fixed Charges—Insurance	Rent, Property Taxes, etc.—Insurance on Bldg. & Contents
Contract Cleaning	Rooms—Contract Cleaning	Rooms—Contract Cleaning
Contract Cleaning—Dining Rooms		F&B—Contract Cleaning
Contract Cleaning—Fumigation	Rooms—Contract Cleaning	Rooms; F&B—Contract Cleaning
Contract Cleaning—Lobbies	Rooms—Contract Cleaning	Rooms—Contract Cleaning
Contract Cleaning—Windows	Rooms—Contract Cleaning	Rooms; F&B—Contract Cleaning
Contract Disinfecting	Rooms—Contract Cleaning	Rooms; F&B—Contract Cleaning
Contract Entertainment		F&B—Music & Entertainment
Contract Exterminating	Rooms—Contract Cleaning	Rooms—Contract Cleaning
Contributions	General—Misc.	A&G—Misc.
Contributions—Convention Bureau	General—Mktg.	Mktg.—Public Relations & Publicity
Controller's Reports	General—Prtg., Stat. & Post.	A&G—Prtg. & Stat.

112

Items	No Restaurant Operation	Restaurant Operation
Convention Bureau	General—Mktg.	Mktg.—Public Relations & Publicity
Convention Office—Contributions	General—Mktg.	Mktg.—Public Relations & Publicity
Cooking Utensils (In Kitchenette Apt.)	Rooms—Misc.	Rooms—Misc.
Coolers—Fiber		F&B—Operating Supplies
Copyright Licenses		A&G; F&B—Licenses
Cord	Rooms—Operating Expenses	Rooms; F&B; etc.—Operating Supplies
Cord for Draperies	POM&E—R&M	POM&E—Furniture, Fixtures, Equip. & Decor
Corking Equipment		F&B—Other Operating Expenses
Corkscrews		F&B—Other Operating Expenses
Corkscrews (Guest)	Rooms—Operating Supplies	Rooms—Operating Supplies
Corn Holders		F&B—China, Glass, Silver & Linen
Corsages (Guest)	Rooms—Operating Supplies	Rooms; F&B—Operating Supplies
Cosmetics	Rooms—Operating Supplies	Rooms; F&B; etc.—Operating Supplies
Cost Accounting—Food		A&G—Professional Fees
Cotton, Absorbent	Employee Benefits	Employee Benefits—Misc.
Count & Room Sheets	Rooms—Misc.	Rooms—Operating Supplies
Court Fees	General—Professional Fees	A&G—Professional Fees
Covering—Bureau	POM&E—R&M	POM&E—Furniture, Fixtures, Equip. & Decor
Creamers		F&B—China, Glass, Silver & Linen
Credit Card Commissions	General—Misc.	A&G—Commission Credit Card Charges—Net
Credit & Collection Expenses	General—Misc.	A&G—Misc.
Credit Information Books	General—Misc.	A&G—Misc.
Credit Reports	General—Misc.	A&G—Misc.
Cruets—Liquor Serving		F&B—China, Glass, Silver & Linen
Cretonnes	POM&E—R&M	POM&E—Furniture, Fixtures, Equip. & Decor
Cups—Boullion		F&B—China, Glass, Silver, & Linen
Cups—Coffee		F&B—China, Glass, Silver, & Linen
Cups—Custard		F&B—China, Glass, Silver & Linen
Cups—Paper		F&B—Operating Supplies
Cups—Paper (Employees)	General—Misc.	Rooms; F&B; etc.—Other Operating Expenses
Cups—Paper (Guest)	Rooms—Operating Supplies	Rooms—Operating Supplies
Cups—Tea		F&B—China, Glass, Silver & Linen
Curtain Cleaning	Rooms—Laundry & Dry Clean.	Rooms; F&B—Laundry & Dry Clean
Curtain, Drapery & Scarf Repairs	POM&E—R&M	POM&E—Furniture, Fixtures, Equip. & Decor
Curtain Linings	POM&E—R&M	POM&E—Furniture, Fixtures, Equip. & Decor

Items	No Restaurant Operation	Restaurant Operation
Curtain Poles	POM&E—R&M	POM&E—Furniture, Fixtures, Equip. & Decor
Curtain Repairs	POM&E—R&M	POM&E—Furniture, Fixtures, Equip. & Decor
Curtain Rings	POM&E—R&M	POM&E—Furniture, Fixtures, Equip. & Decor
Curtain Rods	POM&E—R&M	POM&E—Furniture, Fixtures, Equip. & Decor
Curtains—Lace	POM&E—R&M	POM&E—Furniture, Fixtures, Equip. & Decor
Curtains—Shower	Rooms—China, Glassware & Linen	Rooms—China, Glassware & Linen
Custard Cups		F&B—China, Glass, Silver & Linen
Cut Flowers	Rooms—Misc.	Rooms; F&B—Other Operating Expenses
Cuts	General—Mktg.	Mktg.—Adv.—Other Adv. Expenses
Cylinder Oil	POM&E—Operating Supplies & Misc.	POM&E—Engineering Supplies

D

Items	No Restaurant Operation	Restaurant Operation
Daily Reports	General—Prtg., Stat. & Post.	A&G—Prtg. & Stat.
Damaged Articles—Guest	General—Misc.	A&G—Misc.
Dance Licenses		F&B—Licenses
Data Processing—Rent	Fixed Charges—Rent	Rent, Property Taxes, etc.— Rent—EDP Equip.
Data Processing—Supplies	General—Prtg., Stat. & Post.	A&G—Data Processing Expense
Decorating & Painting	POM&E—R&M	POM&E—Furniture, Fixtures, Equip. & Decor
Decorations	Rooms—Misc.	Rooms; F&B—Other Operating Expenses
Delivery Charges on Beverages		F&B—Cost of Food Consumed
Delivery Charges on Food		F&B—Cost of Food Consumed
Deodorants	Rooms—Operating Supplies	Rooms; F&B—Operating Supplies
Depreciation—Building	Fixed Charges—Depr.	Depr. & Amort.—Depr.— Building & Improvements
Depreciation—Equipment	Fixed Charges—Depr.	Depr. & Amort.—Depr.— Furnishings, Fixtures & Equip.
Desk Pad Holders	General—Prtg., Stat. & Post.	Rooms; F&B; etc.—Operating Supplies; A&G— Prtg. & Stat.
Desk Pads (Employee)	General—Prtg., Stat. & Post.	Rooms; F&B; etc.—Operating Supplies; A&G— Prtg. & Stat.
Desk Pads (Guest)	Rooms—Operating Supplies	Rooms—Operating Supplies
Detective Service—Special	General—Misc.	A&G—Misc.
Detergents	Rooms—Operating Supplies	Rooms; F&B—Operating Supplies
Dictograph Rental	General—Misc.	A&G—Misc.
Direct Mail Expenses— Outside Service	General—Mktg.	Mktg.—Other Selling & Promotion Expenses
Directional Signs (Inside Bldg.)	General—Mktg.	Mktg.—Merchandising

Items	No Restaurant Operation	Restaurant Operation
Directories—Rooms	Rooms—Misc.	Rooms—Other Operating Expenses
Directories—Telephone (Out of Town)	Rooms—Misc.	Telephone—Other Operating Expenses
Directors' Expense	General—Misc.	A&G—Misc.
Directors' Fees	General—Misc.	A&G—Misc.
Directory Advertising	General—Mktg.	Mktg.—Adv.—Print
Directory Holders—Telephone	Rooms—Misc.	Telephone—Other Operating Expenses
Dishes—China		F&B—China, Glass, Silver & Linen
Dishes—Glass		F&B—China, Glass, Silver & Linen
Dishes—Silver		F&B—China, Glass, Silver & Linen
Dishwasher Repairs		POM&E—Elec. & Mech. Equip.
Disinfectants	Rooms—Operating Supplies	Rooms; F&B—Operating Supplies
Disinfecting (On Contract)	Rooms—Contract Cleaning	Rooms; F&B—Contract Cleaning
Doilies—Linen	Rooms—China, Glassware & Linen	Rooms—China, Glassware & Linen; F&B—China, Glass, Silver & Linen
Doilies—Paper		F&B—Operating Supplies
Donations	General—Misc.	A&G—Misc.
Door Hangings	POM&E—R&M	POM&E—Furniture, Fixtures, Equip. & Decor
Door Repairs	POM&E—R&M	POM&E—Building
Doubtful Accounts—Provision for	General—Misc.	A&G—Provision for Doubtful Accounts
Down	POM&E—R&M	POM&E—Furniture, Fixtures, Equip. & Decor
Drapery Cleaning	Rooms—Laundry & Dry Cleaning	Rooms; F&B—Laundry & Dry Cleaning
Drapery Cords	POM&E—R&M	POM&E—Furniture, Fixtures, Equip. & Decor
Drapery Linings	POM&E—R&M	POM&E—Furniture, Fixtures, Equip. & Decor
Drapery Repairs	POM&E—R&M	POM&E—Furniture, Fixtures, Equip. & Decor
Dresser Drawer Liners	Rooms—Operating Supplies	Rooms—Operating Supplies
Dresser Tops — Glass	POM&E—R&M	POM&E—Furniture, Fixtures, Equip. & Decor
Dresser Tops — Linen	Rooms—China, Glassware & Linen	Rooms—China, Glassware & Linen
Dresses	Rooms—Uniforms	Rooms; F&B; House Laundry—Uniforms
Drinking Glasses	Rooms—China, Glassware & Linen	Rooms—China, Glassware & Linen; F&B—China, Glass, Silver & Linen
Drugs—Employees	Employee Benefits	Employee Benefits—Misc.
Drugs & Other Medical Supplies—Guests	Rooms—Operating Supplies	Rooms; F&B—Operating Supplies

Items	No Restaurant Operation	Restaurant Operation
Dry Cleaning	Rooms—Laundry & Dry Cleaning	Rooms; F&B—Laundry & Dry Cleaning
Dry Ice	Rooms—Operating Supplies	F&B—Operating Supplies
Duck		House Laundry—Laundry Supplies
Dues—Hotel Association	General—Trade Assn. Dues & Trade Publications	A&G—Trade Assn. Dues & Trade Publications
Dues—Association (Marketing Employees)	General—Mktg.	Mktg.—Other Selling and Promotional Expenses
Duplicating & Copying Service	General—Prtg., Stat. & Post.	A&G—Misc.
Dust Brushes	Rooms—Operating Supplies	Rooms; F&B—Operating Supplies
Dust Cloths	Rooms—Operating Supplies	Rooms; F&B—Operating Supplies
Dust Pans	Rooms—Operating Supplies	Rooms; F&B—Operating Supplies
Dusters	Rooms—Operating Supplies	Rooms; F&B—Operating Supplies
Dye for Carpets & Rugs	POM&E—R&M	POM&E—Furniture, Fixtures, Equip. & Decor
Dynamo Repairs	POM&E—R&M	POM&E—Elec. & Mech. Equip.

E

Items	No Restaurant Operation	Restaurant Operation
Ecru		House Laundry—Laundry Supplies
Educational Activities for Employees	Employee Benefits	Employee Benefits—Misc.
Educational Books & Pamphlets for Employees	Employee Benefits	Employee Benefits—Misc.
Egg Beaters		F&B—Other Operating Expenses
Electric Breakdown Service	POM&E—R&M	POM&E—Elec. & Mech. Equip.
Electric Bulbs	POM&E—Operating Supplies & Misc.	POM&E—Operating Supplies
Electric Current	POM&E—Electricity	POM&E—Electric Current
Electric Fan Repairs	POM&E—R&M	POM&E—Elec. & Mech. Equip.
Electric Fixture Repairs	POM&E—R&M	POM&E—Elec. & Mech. Equip.
Electric Sign Maintenance Contract	POM&E—R&M	POM&E—Elec. & Mech. Equip.
Electrical & Mechanical Repairs	POM&E—R&M	POM&E—Elec. & Mech. Equip.
Electrical System Repairs	POM&E—R&M	POM&E—Elec. & Mech. Equip.
Electricity—Cooking		F&B—Kitchen Fuel
Electricity for Refrigeration (in Kitchenette Apts.)	Rooms—Misc.	Rooms—Other Operating Expenses
Electros	General—Mktg.	Mktg.—Adv.—Print
Elevator Cables	POM&E—R&M	POM&E—Elec. & Mech. Equip.
Elevator Inspection Service	POM&E—R&M	POM&E—Elec. & Mech. Equip.

Items	No Restaurant Operation	Restaurant Operation
Elevator Liability Insurance	General—Insurance—General	A&G—Insurance—General
Elevator Licenses	POM&E—Operating Supplies & Misc.	POM&E—Misc.
Elevator Repairs	POM&E—R&M	POM&E—Elec. & Mech. Equip.
Emergency Rooms Slips	Rooms—Operating Supplies	Rooms—Operating Supplies
Employee Housing	Employee Benefits	Employee Benefits—Misc.
Employee Investigations	General—Misc.	A&G—Misc.
Employee Relations Expense	Employee Benefits	Employee Benefits—Misc.
Employee Transportation	Rooms—Misc.	Rooms—Other Operating Expenses
Employees' Bonuses	Rooms—Salaries & Wages	Rooms; F&B; etc. — Salaries & Wages
Employees' Clinic (Medical Aid)	Employee Benefits	Employee Benefits—Misc.
Employees' Credit Union	Employee Benefits	Employee Benefits—Misc.
Employees' Lodging	Employee Benefits	Employee Benefits—Misc.
Employees' Magazines	Employee Benefits	Employee Benefits—Misc.
Employees' Meals	Employee Benefits	Rooms; F&B; etc.— Employee Benefits
Enamel	POM&E—R&M	POM&E—Painting & Decorating
Engineering Licenses	POM&E—Operating Supplies & Misc.	POM&E—Misc.
Engineering Supplies	POM&E—Operating Supplies & Misc.	POM&E—Engineering Supplies
Engineer's Report Forms	POM&E—Operating Supplies & Misc.	POM&E—Operating Supplies
Entertainers—Professional		F&B—Music & Entertainment
Entertaining—Complimentary at Hotel	General—Mktg.	Mktg.—Sales—Other Selling Expenses
Entertainment and Music		F&B—Music & Entertainment
Entertainment Programs		F&B—Music & Entertainment
Envelope Addressing	General—Mktg.	Mktg.—Other Selling & Promotional Expenses
Envelopes	General—Prtg., Stat. & Post.; Rooms—Operating Supplies	Rooms—Operating Supplies; A&G—Prtg. & Stat.
Envelopes—Guest	Rooms—Operating Supplies	Rooms—Operating Supplies
Envelopes—Safety	Rooms—Operating Supplies	Rooms—Operating Supplies
Envelopes—Telephone Messages	Rooms—Operating Supplies	Telephone—Prtg. & Stat.
Equipment & Belts— Window Cleaners	Rooms—Operating Supplies	Rooms; F&B—Operating Supplies
Equipment Charges— Telephone	General—Telephone & Telegrams	Telephone—Rental of Equip.
Equipment Rental	Fixed Charges—Rent	Rent, Property Taxes, etc.— Rent—Furnishings, Fixtures & Equip.
Eradicators (Ink)	General—Prtg., Stat. & Post.	Rooms; F&B; etc.— Operating Supplies
Erasers	General—Prtg., Stat. & Post.	Rooms; F&B; etc.— Operating Supplies
Erusticator		House Laundry—Laundry Supplies

Items	No Restaurant Operation	Restaurant Operation
Exchange on Bank Checks & Currency	General—Misc.	A&G—Misc.
Executive Office Expenses	General—Misc.	A&G—Misc.
Expositions—Local	General—Mktg.	Mktg.—Public Relations & Publicity
Express Charges	General—Misc.	A&G—Misc.
Express Charges on Beverages		F&B—Cost of Bev. Sold
Express Charges on Food		F&B—Cost of Food Consumed
Exterminating (On Contract)	Rooms—Contract Cleaning	Rooms; F&B—Contract Cleaning

F

Items	No Restaurant Operation	Restaurant Operation
Face Cloths (Guest)	Rooms—Operating Supplies	Rooms—Operating Supplies
Facial Tissues & Holders	Rooms—Operating Supplies	Rooms—Operating Supplies
Fairs—Local	General—Mktg.	Mktg.—Public Relations & Publicity
Fan Repairs—Electric	POM&E—R&M	POM&E—Elec. & Mech. Equip.
Fans—Paper & Straw (Guest)	Rooms—Operating Supplies	Rooms; F&B—Operating Supplies
Fares—Taxicabs—Local	General—Misc.	A&G—Misc.
Favors		F&B; Operating Supplies
Feathers	POM&E—R&M	POM&E—Furniture, Fixtures, Equip. & Decor
Federal Income Taxes	Income Taxes	Federal & State Income Taxes—Federal—Current or Deferred
Federal Retirement Taxes	Employee Benefits	Employee Benefits—Federal Retirement
Federal Unemployment Taxes	Employee Benefits	Employee Benefits—Federal Unemployment
Felt	POM&E—R&M	POM&E—Furniture, Fixtures, Equip. & Decor
Felt Padding		House Laundry—Laundry Supplies
Felt Padding—Furniture	POM&E—R&M	POM&E—Furniture, Fixtures, Equip. & Decor
Ferns	Rooms—Misc.	Rooms; F&B—Other Operating Expenses
Fiber Coolers		F&B—Operating Supplies
Fiber Vases	Rooms—Misc.	Rooms; F&B; etc.—Other Operating Expenses
File Cards	General—Prtg., Stat. & Post.	Rooms; F&B; etc.—Operating Supplies
Film Rental		F&B—Music & Entertainment
Films		F&B—Music & Entertainment
Filter Paper		F&B—Operating Supplies
Fines	General—Misc.	A&G—Misc.
Fire Alarm Service	General—Misc.	A&G—Misc.
Fire Axes	General—Misc.	A&G—Misc.
Fire Bucket Sand	General—Misc.	A&G—Misc.
Fire Escape Repairs	POM&E—R&M	POM&E—Building
Fire Extinguisher Chemicals	General—Misc.	A&G—Misc.
Fire Hose Repairs	POM&E—R&M	POM&E—Building
Firewood—Rooms & Lobby	Rooms—Misc.	Rooms—Other Operating Expenses
First Aid Supplies	Employee Benefits	Employee Benefits—Misc.

Items	No Restaurant Operation	Restaurant Operation
Fixture Repairs—Electric ...	POM&E—R&M	POM&E—Elec. & Mech. Equip.
Flag & Bunting	Rooms—Misc.	Rooms; F&B; etc.—Other Operating Expenses
Flashlight & Batteries	POM&E—Operating Supplies & Misc.	POM&E—Operating Supplies
Flatware		F&B—China, Glass, Silver & Linen
Floor Covering Repairs	POM&E—R&M	POM&E—Furniture, Fixtures, Equip. & Decor
Floor Padding	POM&E—R&M	POM&E—Furniture, Fixtures, Equip. & Decor
Floor Plans	Rooms—Operating Supplies .	Rooms—Operating Supplies
Floor Polish	Rooms—Operating Supplies .	Rooms; F&B—Operating Supplies
Floor Repairs	POM&E—R&M	POM&E—Building
Floor Soap	Rooms—Operating Supplies .	Rooms; F&B—Operating Supplies
Floor Wax	Rooms—Operating Supplies .	Rooms; F&B—Operating Supplies
Flower Pots	Rooms—Misc.	Rooms; F&B—Other Operating Expenses
Flowers—Artificial	Rooms—Misc.	Rooms; F&B—Other Operating Expenses
Flowers—Cut	Rooms—Misc.	Rooms; F&B—Other Operating Expenses
Flowers—Guest	Rooms—Operating Supplies .	Rooms—Operating Supplies
Fluids—Cleaning	Rooms—Operating Supplies .	Rooms; F&B—Operating Supplies
Fly Paper	Rooms—Operating Supplies .	Rooms; F&B—Operating Supplies
Fly Swatters	Rooms—Operating Supplies .	Rooms; F&B—Operating Supplies
Foil Wrapping		F&B—Operating Supplies
Food & Beverage Checking Machines—Repairs & Maintenance		POM&E—Elec. & Mech. Equip.
Food & Beverage Checking Supplies		F&B—Operating Supplies
Food Cost Accounting		A&G—Professional Fees
Food—Gratis (Not Used in the Preparation of Mixed Drinks)		F&B—Operating Supplies
Food Inspection		F&B—Other Operating Expenses
Food Licenses		F&B—Licenses
Food—for Resale	Cost of Food Purchased & Incidental Expenses	F&B—Cost of Food Consumed
Food Truck Repairs		POM&E—Elec. & Mech. Equip.
Food Warmer Supplies	Cost of Food Purchased & Incidental Expenses	F&B—Kitchen Fuel
Foreign Publication Advertising	General—Mktg.	Mktg.—Adv.—Print
Forks—Kitchen		F&B—Other Operating Expenses
Forks—Silver		F&B—China, Glass, Silver & Linen

Items	No Restaurant Operation	Restaurant Operation
Forms—Printed	Rooms—Misc.; General—Prtg., Stat. & Post.	Rooms; F&B; etc.—Operating Supplies; A&G—Prtg. & Stat.
Forms—Report	Rooms—Operating Supplies	Rooms; F&B; etc.—Operating Supplies
Fountain Pens	General—Prtg., Stat. & Post.	A&G—Prtg. & Stat.; Rooms; F&B—Operating Supplies
Frames, Picture	POM&E—R&M	POM&E—Furniture, Fixtures, Equip. & Decor
Franchise Fees	General—Mktg.	Mktg.—Fees & Commission —Franchise Fees
Franchise Taxes	Fixed Charges—State Fixed Franchise Tax	State and Federal Taxes—State Franchise Tax
Freight Charges	General—Misc.	A&G—Misc.
Front Desk Signs	Rooms—Misc.	Rooms—Other Operating Expenses
Fruit (Guest)	Rooms—Operating Supplies	Rooms—Operating Supplies
Fuel	POM&E—Fuel	POM&E—Fuel
Fuel for Cooking—Alcohol		F&B—Kitchen Fuel
Fuel—Gas	POM&E—Fuel	POM&E—Fuel
Fuel—Kitchen		F&B—Kitchen Fuel
Fuel—Oil	POM&E—Fuel	POM&E—Fuel
Fumigation (On Contract)	Rooms—Contract Cleaning	Rooms; F&B—Contract Cleaning
Fumigators	Rooms—Operating Supplies	Rooms; F&B—Operating Supplies
Furniture Coverings—Cleaning	Rooms—Laundry & Dry Cleaning	Rooms; F&B—Laundry & Dry Cleaning
Furniture Polish	Rooms—Operating Supplies	Rooms; F&B—Operating Supplies
Furniture Rental (Public Rooms)	Rooms—Misc.	Rooms—Other Operating Expenses
Furniture Repairs	POM&E—R&M	POM&E—Furniture, Fixtures, Equip. & Decor
Fuses	POM&E—Operating Supplies & Misc.	POM&E—Engineering Supplies

G

Items	No Restaurant Operation	Restaurant Operation
Galax Leaves		F&B—Other Operating Expenses
Garage	Rooms—Other Operating Expenses	Rooms; F&B; etc.—Other Operating Expenses
Garbage Cans		F&B—Other Operating Expenses
Garbage Removal	POM&E—Operating Supplies & Misc.	POM&E—Removal of Waste Matter
Garment Bags (Guest)	Rooms—Operating Supplies	Rooms—Operating Supplies
Garment Hangers (Guest)	Rooms—Operating Supplies	Rooms—Operating Supplies
Gas—Carbonated	Cost of Food Purchased & Incidental Expenses	F&B—Cost of Beverage Sales
Gas—Cooking		F&B—Kitchen Fuel
Gas for Refrigeration	POM&E—Operating Supplies & Misc.	POM&E—Misc.

Items	*No Restaurant Operation*	*Restaurant Operation*
Gas for Refrigeration (In Kitchenette Apartments) ..	Rooms—Misc.	Rooms—Other Operating Expenses
Gas—Fuel	POM&E—Fuel	POM&E—Fuel
Gas Governors (Kitchen)		F&B—Kitchen Fuel
Gas (In Kitchenette Apts.) ...	Rooms—Misc.	Rooms—Other Operating Expenses
Gas Range Rentals	Fixed Charges—Rent	F&B—Other Operating Expenses
Gas Range Repairs (In Kitchenette Apartments) ..	POM&E—R&M	POM&E—Furniture, Fixtures, Equip. & Decor
Gasoline—Cleaning	Rooms—Operating Supplies .	Rooms; F&B—Operating Supplies
Gasoline—Motor Vehicles ..	Rooms—Misc.; General—Traveling Expenses	Rooms—Other Operating Expenses; A&G—Traveling Expenses
Gasoline—for Resale	Cost of Gas, Oil, Auto Supplies Purchased	Gas Station—Cost of Sales
Generator Brushes	POM&E—R&M	POM&E—Elec. & Mech. Equip.
Generator Repairs	POM&E—R&M	POM&E—Elec. & Mech. Equip.
Gifts (Guest)	Rooms—Operating Supplies .	Rooms; F&B—Operating Supplies
Glass Bowls		F&B—China, Glass, Silver & Linen
Glass Dishes		F&B—China, Glass, Silver & Linen
Glass—Dresser & Table Tops	POM&E—R&M	POM&E—Furniture, Fixtures, Equip. & Decor
Glass for Furniture Repairs ..	POM&E—R&M	POM&E—Furniture, Fixures, Equip. & Decor
Glass Pitchers	Rooms—China, Glass & Linen	Rooms—China, Glass & Linen; F&B—China, Glass, Silver & Linen
Glass Trays	Rooms—China, Glass & Linen	Rooms—China, Glass & Linen; F&B—China, Glass, Silver & Linen
Glass Stirrers—Beverages ...		F&B—Other Operating Expenses
Glasses—Drinking	Rooms—China, Glass & Linen	Rooms—China, Glass & Linen; F&B—China, Glass, Silver & Linen
Glasses—Water	Rooms—China, Glass & Linen	Rooms—China, Glass & Linen; F&B—China, Glass, Silver & Linen
Glassine Envelopes	General—Prtg., Stat. & Post.	A&G—Prtg. & Stat.
Glassware	Rooms—China, Glass & Linen	Rooms—China, Glass & Linen; F&B—China, Glass & Linen; Gift Shop—Operating Supp.
Glassware—Liquor (Cocktail, Highball, Wine, etc.)		F&B—China, Glass, Silver & Linen
Glazing (Replacing Window Glass)	POM&E—R&M	POM&E—Building
Gloves	Rooms—Uniforms	Rooms; F&B—Uniforms

Items	No Restaurant Operation	Restaurant Operation
Glue—Office	General—Prtg., Stat. & Post.	Rooms; F&B; etc.—Operating Supplies; A&G—Prtg. & Stat.
Glue—Painting & Decorating	POM&E—R&M	POM&E—Furniture, Fixtures, Equip. & Decor
Goblets—Water		F&B—China, Glass, Silver & Linen
Goldfish	Rooms—Misc.	Rooms; F&B—Other Operating Expenses
Gold Leaf	POM&E—R&M	POM&E—Furniture, Fixtures, Equip. & Decor
Governors—Gas		F&B—Kitchen Fuel
Gratis Food (Not Used in the Preparation of Mixed Drinks)		F&B—Operating Supplies
Gratuities & Christmas Presents (Other Than Employees or Guests)	General—Misc.	A&G—Misc.
Grease	POM&E—Operating Supplies & Misc.	POM&E—Engineering Supplies
Grease—Hotel Vehicles	POM&E—Operating Supplies & Misc.	Garage—Parking Lot—Operating Supplies
Greatcoats—Doormen	Rooms—Uniforms	Rooms—Uniforms
Greeting Cards	General—Mktg.	Mktg.—Merchandising
Gross Receipt Taxes	Fixed Charges—Taxes	Rent, Prop. Taxes, etc.—Property Taxes, etc.—Other
Ground Rent	Fixed Charges—Rent	Rent, Property Taxes, etc.—Rent—Real Estate
Grounds Expense	POM&E—R&M	POM&E—Grounds & Landscaping
Guest History Analysis Regular	General—Mktg.	Mktg.—Research
Guest Ledgers	General—Prtg., Stat. & Post.	A&G—Prtg. & Stat.
Guest Registers	Rooms—Misc.	Rooms—Operating Supplies
Guest Soap	Rooms—Operating Supplies	Rooms—Operating Supplies
Guest Stationery	Rooms—Operating Supplies	Rooms—Operating Supplies
Guest Transportation	Rooms—Other Operating Expenses	Rooms—Other Operating Expenses
Guide Book Advertising	General—Mktg.	Mktg.—Adv.—Print
Guides	General—Mktg.	Mktg.—Merchandising
Guides—Tourist	General—Mktg.	Mktg.—Merchandising

H

Items	No Restaurant Operation	Restaurant Operation
Hair Nets (Guest)	Rooms—Operating Supplies	Rooms—Operating Supplies
Hairpins (Guest)	Rooms—Operating Supplies	Rooms—Operating Supplies
Hangers (Guest)	Rooms—Operating Supplies	Rooms—Operating Supplies
Hangings Repair	POM&E—R&M	POM&E—Furniture, Fixtures, Equip. & Decor
Head Bands	Rooms—Uniforms	Rooms; F&B—Uniforms
Heating Plant Repairs	POM&E—R&M	POM&E—Elec. & Mech. Equip.
Help Wanted Ads	General Expense—Misc.	Rooms; F&B; etc.—Other Operating Expenses
Hire of Automobiles	General—Traveling Expenses	A&G—Traveling Expenses; Mktg.—Other Selling & Promotional Expenses

Items	No Restaurant Operation	Restaurant Operation
Hire of Furniture (Public Rooms) Banquet		F&B—Other Operating Expenses
Non-Banquet	Rooms—Misc.	Rooms—Other Operating Expenses
Holders—Chop		F&B—Operating Supplies
Holders—Corn		F&B—China, Glass, Silver & Linen
Holders — Paper		F&B—Operating Supplies
Hooks	POM&E—Operating Supplies & Misc.	POM&E—Misc.
Hotel Association Dues	General—Trade Assn. Dues & Trade Subscriptions	A&G— Trade Assn. Dues & Trade Subscriptions
Hotel Sales Management Association Dues	General—Mktg.	Mktg.—Other Selling & Promotion Expense
Housekeeper & Maids' Reports	Rooms—Operating Supplies .	Rooms—Operating Supplies
House Floor Plans (for Outside Mailing)	General—Mktg.	Mktg.—Merchandising
House Publication (for Employees)	Employee Benefits	Employee Benefits—Misc.
House Publication (for Group Distribution)	General—Mktg.	Mktg.—Merchandising
Housing—Employees	General—Misc.	A&G—Misc.

I

Items	No Restaurant Operation	Restaurant Operation
Ice		F&B—Operating Supplies
Ice (In Kitchenette Apts.) ...	Rooms—Misc.	Rooms—Other Operating Expenses
Ice Machine Repairs	POM&E—R&M	POM&E—Elec. & Mech. Equip.
Ice Picks		F&B—Other Operating Expenses
Ice Tongs—Bar		F&B—Other Operating Expenses
Icing Sugar Decorations		F&B—Other Operating Expenses
Incinerator Operation	POM&E—Operating Supplies & Misc.	POM&E—Removal of Waste Matter
Incinerator Repairs	POM&E—R&M	POM&E—Elec. & Mech. Equip.
Income Taxes—Federal	Fixed Charges—Federal Income Tax	Federal & State Income Taxes—Federal—Current or Deferred
Index Cards	Rooms—Operating Supplies; General—Prtg., Stat. & Post.	Rooms; F&B; etc.— Operating Supplies
Indexes	Rooms—Operating Supplies; General—Prtg., Stat. & Post.	Rooms; F&B; etc.— Operating Supplies
Ink (Employees)	General—Prtg., Stat. & Post.	Rooms; F&B; etc.— Operating Supplies; A&G— Prtg. & Stat.
Ink Eradicator	General—Prtg., Stat. & Post.	Rooms; F&B; etc.— Operating Supplies

Items	*No Restaurant Operation*	*Restaurant Operation*
Ink (Guest)	Rooms—Operating Supplies	Rooms—Operating Supplies
Ink Pads (Employee)	General—Prtg., Stat. & Post.	Rooms; F&B; etc.— Operating Supplies; A&G— Prtg. & Stat.
Inkwells (Employee)	General—Prtg., Stat. & Post.	Rooms; F&B; etc.— Operating Supplies; A&G— Prtg. & Stat.
Inkwells (Guest)	Rooms—Operating Supplies .	Rooms—Operating Supplies
Insecticides	Rooms—Operating Supplies .	Rooms; F&B—Operating Supplies
Inspection—Mechanical	POM&E—R&M	POM&E—Elec. & Mech. Equip.
Instrument Board Repairs ...	POM&E—R&M	POM&E—Elec. & Mech. Equip.
Insurance—Boiler Explosion	Fixed Charges—Fire Ins.	Rent, Property Taxes, etc.— Insurance of Bldg. & Contents
Insurance—Boiler Liability ..	General—Insurance—General	A&G—Insurance—General
Insurance—Building & Contents	Fixed Charges—Fire Ins.	Rent, Property Taxes, etc.— Insurance on Bldg. & Contents
Insurance—Burglary	General—Insurance	A&G—Insurance—General
Insurance—Business Interruption	General—Insurance	A&G—Insurance—General
Insurance—Contents of Building	Fixed Charges—Fire Ins.	Rent, Property Taxes, etc.— Insurance on Bldg. & Contents
Insurance—Elevator Liability	General—Insurance	A&G—Insurance—General
Insurance—Employees' Liability	Employee Benefits	Employee Benefits— Workmen's Compensation Insurance
Insurance—Fidelity Bonds ..	General—Insurance	A&G—Insurance—General
Insurance—Fire	Fixed Charges—Fire Ins.	Rent, Property Taxes, etc.— Insurance on Bldg. & Contents
Insurance—Flywheel Liability	General—Insurance	A&G—Insurance—General
Insurance—Forgery	General—Insurance	A&G—Insurance—General
Insurance—Fraud	General—Insurance	A&G—Insurance—General
Insurance—Furniture & Equipment	Fixed Charges—Insurance ..	Rent, Prop. Taxes, etc.— Insurance on Bldg. & Contents
Insurance—Group (Non-Union)	Employee Benefits	Employee Benefits— Non-Union Insurance
Insurance—Group (Union) ..	Employee Benefits	Employee Benefits— Union Insurance
Insurance—Holdup	General—Insurance	A&G—Insurance—General
Insurance—Hospitalization— (Non-Union Employees) ..	Employee Benefits	Employee Benefits— Non-Union Insurance
Insurance—Hospitalization— (Union Employees)	Employee Benefits	Employee Benefits— Union Insurance
Insurance—Life (Employee Beneficiary) ...	General—Insurance	A&G—Insurance—General

124

Items	No Restaurant Operation	Restaurant Operation
Insurance—Life—Union Employee (Employee Beneficiary)	Employee Benefits	Employee Benefits—Union Insurance
Insurance—Legal Liability	General—Insurance	A&G—Insurance—General
Insurance—Lost & Damaged Articles	General—Insurance	A&G—Insurance—General
Insurance—Motor Vehicle	General—Insurance	A&G—Insurance—General
Insurance—Non-Ownership, Auto	General—Insurance	A&G—Insurance—General
Insurance—Occupational Disease	Employee Benefits	Employee Benefits—Workmen's Compensation Insurance
Insurance—Off-Duty—Accident—Union Emp.	Employee Benefits	Employee Benefits—Union Insurance
Insurance—Off-Duty Insurance (Non-Union Employees)	Employee Benefits	Employee Benefits—Non-Union Insurance
Insurance—Parcel Post	General—Insurance	A&G—Insurance—General
Insurance—Plate Glass Breakage	Fixed Charges—Fire Ins.	Rent, Property Taxes, etc.—Insurance on Bldg. & Contents
Insurance—Products Liability	General—Insurance	A&G—Insurance—General
Insurance—Public Liability	General—Insurance	A&G—Insurance—General
Insurance—Rent	General—Insurance	A&G—Insurance—General
Insurance—Robbery	General—Insurance	A&G—Insurance—General
Insurance—Sprinkler Leakage	Fixed Charges—Fire Ins.	Rent, Property Taxes, etc.—Ins. on Bldg. & Contents
Insurance—Tornado	Fixed Charges—Fire Ins.	Rent, Property Taxes, etc.—Ins. on Bldg. & Contents
Insurance—Use & Occupancy	General—Insurance	A&G—Insurance—General
Insurance—Vehicles	General—Insurance	A&G—Insurance—General
Insurance—Weather	Fixed Charges—Insurance	Rent, Prop. Taxes, etc.—Ins. on Bldg. & Contents
Insurance—Workmen's Compensation	Employee Benefits	Employee Benefits—Workmen's Compensation Ins.
Interest	Fixed Charges—Interest	Interest Expense—Other Interest
Interest on Bonds	Fixed Charges—Interest	Interest Expense—Other Long-Term Debt
Interest on First Mortgage	Fixed Charges—Interest	Interest Expense—First Mortgage
Interest on Notes	Fixed Charges—Interest	Interest Expense—Notes Payable
Interest on Taxes in Arrears	Fixed Charges—Interest	Interest Expense—Other Interest
Internal Audit Expense	General—Misc.	A&G—Misc.
Internal Audit Fees (Chain Motels)	General—Misc.	A&G—Misc.
Internal Communicating Systems	General—Misc.	A&G—Misc.
Investigation of Employees	General—Misc.	A&G—Misc.

J

Jumpers	Rooms—Uniforms	Rooms; F&B; etc.—Uniforms

Items	No Restaurant Operation	Restaurant Operation
K		
Kettles		F&B—Other Operating Expenses
Key Pouches	Rooms—Uniforms	Rooms—Uniforms
Key Repairs	POM&E—R&M	POM&E—Elec. & Mech. Equip.
Keys for Safe-Deposit Boxes	Rooms—Misc.	Rooms—Other Operating Expenses
Key Tag Repairs	POM&E—R&M	POM&E—Elec. & Mech. Equip.
Kitchen Equip. Repairs		POM&E—Elec. & Mech. Equip.
Kitchenette Expenses	Rooms—Misc.	Rooms—Other Operating Expenses
Kitchen Forks		F&B—Other Operating Expenses
Kitchen Fuel		F&B—Kitchen Fuel
Kitchen Knives		F&B—Other Operating Expenses
Kitchen Ladles		F&B—Other Operating Expenses
Kitchen Spoons		F&B—Other Operating Expenses
Kitchen Utensils		F&B—Other Operating Expenses
Klingerit Packing	POM&E—Operating Supplies & Misc.	POM&E—Engineering Supplies
Knife Sharpening		F&B—Other Operating Expenses
Knives—Oyster		F&B—Other Operating Expenses
Knives—Silver		F&B—China, Glass, Silver & Linen
L		
Laboratory Costs	POM&E—Operating Supplies & Misc.	F&B—Other Operating Expenses; POM&E—Misc.
Lace Curtains	POM&E—R&M	POM&E—Furniture, Fixtures, Equip. & Decor
Lacquer	POM&E—R&M	POM&E—Furniture, Fixtures, Equip. & Decor
Ladders	POM&E—R&M	POM&E—Elec. & Mech. Equip.
Ladles		F&B—China, Glass, Silver, & Linen
Ladles—Kitchen		F&B—Other Operating Expenses
Lamp Shade Cleaning	Rooms—Laundry & Dry Cleaning	Rooms; F&B—Laundry & Dry Cleaning
Landscaping	POM&E—R&M	POM&E—Grounds & Landscaping
Larding Needles		F&B—Other Operating Expenses
Laundry	Rooms—Laundry & Dry Cleaning	Rooms; F&B—Laundry & Dry Cleaning
Laundry Bags	Rooms—Laundry & Dry Cleaning	House Laundry—Laundry Supplies

Items	*No Restaurant Operation*	*Restaurant Operation*
Laundry Boxes		House Laundry—Laundry Supplies
Laundry Envelopes (for Shirts, etc.)		House Laundry—Laundry Supplies
Laundry Lists	Rooms—Laundry & Dry Cleaning	House Laundry—Laundry Supplies
Laundry Plant Repairs	POM&E—R&M	POM&E—Elec. & Mech. Equip.
Laundry Salt		House Laundry—Laundry Supplies
Laundry Supplies	Rooms—Laundry & Dry Cleaning	House Laundry—Laundry Supplies
Laundry Tags		House Laundry—Laundry Supplies
Layouts	General—Mktg.	Mktg.—Adv.—Other Adv. Expenses
Leasehold Amortization	Fixed Charges—Amort. of Leasehold	Depr. & Amort.—Amort.— Leasehold & Improvements
Leasehold Improvements Amortization	Fixed Charges—Amort. of Leasehold Improvements	Depr. & Amort.—Amort.— Leasehold & Improvements
Leather on Uniforms	Rooms—Uniforms	Rooms; F&B—Uniforms
Leaves—Galax		F&B—Other Operating Expenses
Ledgers—Guest	General—Prtg., Stat. & Post.	A&G—Prtg. & Stat.
Legal Expenses	General—Professional Fees .	A&G—Professional Fees
Legal Fees	General—Professional Fees .	A&G—Professional Fees
Lemon Oil	Rooms—Operating Supplies .	Rooms; F&B—Operating Supplies
Lemon Squeezers—Bar		F&B—Other Operating Expenses
Lemon Squeezers—Kitchen .		F&B—Other Operating Expenses
Letter Sealing	General—Mktg.	Mktg.—Other Selling & Promotion Expenses
Letter Service	General—Mktg.	Mktg.—Other Selling & Promotion Expenses
Letter Service—Postage	General—Mktg.	Mktg.—Other Selling & Promotion Expenses
Letter Signing	General—Mktg.	Mktg.—Other Selling & Promotion Expenses
Letter Writing	General—Mktg.	Mktg.—Other Selling & Promotion Expenses
Letters for Bulletin Boards ..	Rooms—Misc.	Rooms; F&B; etc.—Other Operating Expenses; A&G; Telephone—Misc.
Library Paste	General—Prtg., Stat. & Post.	Rooms; F&B; etc.—Operating Expenses; A&G—Prtg. & Stat.
Licenses—Beverages, Federal		F&B—Licenses
Licenses—Beverages, Municipal		F&B—Licenses
Licenses—Beverages, State .		F&B—Licenses
Licenses—Canopy	General—Misc.	A&G—Licenses
Licenses—Checkrooms	General—Misc.	A&G—Licenses

Items	No Restaurant Operation	Restaurant Operation
Licenses—Cigar Stand	General—Misc.	A&G—Licenses
Licenses—Dance		F&B—Licenses
Licenses—Elevator	POM&E—Operating Supplies & Misc.	POM&E—Misc.
Licenses—Engineering, etc.	POM&E—Operating Supplies & Misc.	POM&E—Misc.
Licenses—General	General—Misc.	A&G—Licenses
Licenses—Gift Shop		Gift Shop—Other Operating Expenses
Licenses—Guest Room	Rooms—Misc.	Rooms—Other Operating Expenses
Licenses—Ice Cream		F&B—Licenses
Licenses—Laundry		House Laundry—Misc.
Licenses—Locksmith	POM&E—Operating Supplies & Misc.	POM&E—Misc.
Licenses—Mercantile		F&B; etc.—Licenses
Licenses—Music		F&B—Licenses
Licenses—Public Rooms	Rooms—Misc.	Rooms—Other Operating Expenses
Light—Cost of	POM&E—Electricity	POM&E—Electric Current
Lime Chloride		House Laundry—Laundry Supplies
Lincrusta	POM&E—R&M	POM&E—Elec. & Mech. Equip.
Linen	Rooms—China, Glassware & Linen	Rooms—China, Glassware & Linen; F&B—China, Glass Silver & Linen
Linen Doilies	Rooms—China, Glassware & Linen	Rooms—China, Glassware & Linen; F&B—China, Glass, Silver & Linen
Linen Dresser Tops	Rooms—China, Glassware & Linen	Rooms—China, Glassware & Linen; F&B—China, Glass, Silver & Linen
Linen Napkins		F&B—China, Glass, Silver & Linen
Linen Rental	Rooms—China, Glassware & Linen	Rooms—China, Glassware & Linen; F&B—China, Glass, Silver & Linen
Linen Sheets	Rooms—China, Glassware & Linen	Rooms—China, Glassware & Linen
Linen—Table (Replacement in Kitchenette Apts.)	Rooms—Misc.	Rooms—Other Operating Expenses
Linen Towels	Rooms—China, Glassware & Linen	Rooms—China, Glassware & Linen; F&B—China, Glass, Silver & Linen
Liners—Dresser Drawers	Rooms—Operating Supplies	Rooms—Operating Supplies
Liners—Paper		F&B—Operating Supplies
Linoleum	POM&E—R&M	POM&E—Furniture, Fixtures, Equip. & Decor
Liquid Containers, Paper		F&B—Operating Supplies
Literature—Educational for Employees	Employee Benefits	Employee Benefits—Misc.
Literature—Foreign Distribution	General—Mktg.	Mktg.—Adv.—Print
Literature (Promotional)	General—Mktg.	Mktg.—Merchandising

Items	No Restaurant Operation	Restaurant Operation
Loan Fund Operation— for Employees	Employee Benefits	Employee Benefits—Misc.
Lobby Cleaning (On Contract)	Rooms—Contract Cleaning	Rooms—Contract Cleaning
Lobby Signs	General—Mktg.	Mktg.—Merchandising
Lock Repairs	POM&E—R&M	POM&E—Elec. & Mech. Equip.
Lodging of Employees	General—Misc.	A&G—Misc.
Log Books	Rooms—Misc., General— Prtg., Stat. & Post.	Rooms; F&B—Other Operating Expenses; A&G —Prtg. & Stat.
Loss or Gain on Sale of Property	Gain or Loss on Sale of Prop.	Gain or Loss on Sale of Property
Lost & Damaged Articles (Guest)	General—Misc.	A&G—Misc.
Lost & Found Reports	General—Misc.	A&G—Prtg. & Stat.
Lubricating Oils & Greases	POM&E—Operating Supplies & Misc.	POM&E—Engineering Supplies
Lubricating Oils & Greases (Motor Vehicles)	General—Travel Expense	Garage—Parking Lot— Operating Supplies
Lumber	POM&E—R&M	POM&E—Building
Lye	Rooms—Operating Supplies	Rooms; F&B; etc.— Operating Supplies

M

Items	No Restaurant Operation	Restaurant Operation
Machine Oil	POM&E—Operating Supplies & Misc.	POM&E—Engineering Supplies
Machinery Repairs	POM&E—R&M	POM&E—Elec. & Mech. Equip.
Magazine Advertising	General—Mktg.	Mktg.—Adv.—Print
Magazines (Guest)	Rooms—Operating Supplies	Rooms—Operating Supplies
Magazines—Trade	General—Trade Assn. Dues & Trade Subscriptions	A&G—Trade Assn. Dues & Trade Subscriptions
Maids' Reports	Rooms—Operating Supplies	Rooms—Operating Supplies
Mail Bags	General—Misc.	A&G—Misc.
Mail Chute Rentals	General—Misc.	A&G—Misc.
Mailing Lists	General—Mktg.	Mktg.—Other Selling & Promotion Expenses
Maintenance Contracts— Electric Signs	POM&E—R&M	POM&E—Elec. & Mech. Equip.
Maintenance Contracts— Office Equipment	POM&E—R&M	POM&E—Elec. & Mech. Equip.
Maintenance—Electric Sub-Meters	POM&E—Operating Supplies & Misc.	POM&E—Sale of Electric Current
Management Fees	General—Misc.	A&G—Management Fees
Mangle Aprons		House Laundry—Laundry Supplies
Manuals—Service (Instructional Material)	Employee Benefits	Employee Benefits—Misc.
Maps	General—Mktg.	Mktg.—Merchandising
Markers		F&B—Other Operating Expenses

Items	No Restaurant Operation	Restaurant Operation
Marketing Service Fees	General—Mktg.	Mktg.—Fees & Commissions—Other Fees & Commissions
Marking Ink—Laundry		House Laundry—Laundry Supplies
Marking Ink—Linen Room	Rooms—Misc.	Rooms—Other Operating Expenses
Marquee Licenses	General—Misc.	A&G—Misc.
Marquee Repairs	POM&E—R&M	POM&E—Building
Masonry Repairs	POM&E—R&M	POM&E—Building
Matches (Guest)	Rooms—Operating Supplies	Rooms; F&B;—Operating Supplies
Mats	General—Mktg.	Mktg.—Adv.—Other Adv. Expenses
Mats—Bath	Rooms—China, Glassware & Linen	Rooms—China, Glassware & Linen
Mats—Floor	POM&E—R&M	POM&E—Furniture, Fixtures, Equip. & Decor
Mats—Rubber	POM&E—R&M	POM&E—Furniture, Fixtures, Equip. & Decor
Mattress Protectors	Rooms—China, Glassware & Linen	Rooms—China, Glassware & Linen
Mattress Repairs	POM&E—R&M	POM&E—Furniture, Fixtures, Equip. & Decor
Meals—Employees	Employee Benefits	Rooms; F&B; etc.—Employee Benefits
Mechanical Inspection	POM&E—R&M	POM&E—Elec. & Mech. Equip.
Mechanical Music	Rooms—Misc.	F&B—Music & Enter.
Medical Fees (Service to Employees)	Employee Benefits	Employee Benefits—Misc.
Medical Fees (Service to Guests)	General—Misc.	A&G—Misc.
Medical Supplies (for Employees)	Employee Benefits	Employee Benefits—Misc.
Medical Supplies (for Guests)	General—Misc.	A&G—Misc.
Membership Dues—Motel Associations	General—Trade Assn. Dues & Trade Subscriptions	A&G—Trade Assn. Dues & Trade Subscriptions
Membership Dues—Marketing Employees	General—Mktg.	Mktg.—Other Selling & Promotion Expenses
Menus		F&B—Operating Supplies
Mercantile Agency Subscriptions	General—Misc.	A&G—Misc.
Mercantile Licenses	Cost of Food Purchased & Incidental Expenses	F&B—Licenses
Message Envelopes (Telephone)	General—Prtg., Stat. & Post.	Telephone—Prtg. & Stat.
Metal Parts	POM&E—R&M	POM&E—Elec. & Mech. Equip.; Building, etc.
Metal Polish	Rooms—Operating Supplies	Rooms; F&B—Operating Supplies
Meter Charts	POM&E—Operating Supplies & Misc.	POM&E—Misc.
Meter Rentals	POM&E—Operating Supplies & Misc.	POM&E—Misc.

Items	No Restaurant Operation	Restaurant Operation
Mixer Repairs		POM&E—Elec. & Mech. Equip.
Mixers—Batter		F&B—Other Operating Expenses
Mixers—Beverage		F&B—Other Operating Expenses
Mixing Bowls		F&B—Other Operating Expenses
Mixing Spoons		F&B—Other Operating Expenses
Molds		F&B—Other Operating Expenses
Mop Handles & Wringers ...	Rooms—Operating Supplies .	Rooms; F&B—Operating Supplies
Mops	Rooms—Operating Supplies .	Rooms; F&B—Operating Supplies
Mortgage Interest on First Mortgage	Fixed Charges—Interest	Interest Expense—First Mortgage
Moth-Proofing—Contracts ..	Rooms—Contract Cleaning ..	Rooms: F&B—Contract Cleaning
Moth-Proofing Chemicals ...	Rooms—Operating Supplies .	Rooms; F&B—Operating Supplies
Motor Fuel (for Motor Vehicles)	General—Traveling Expenses	Garage—Parking Lot— Operating Supplies
Motor Repairs	POM&E—R&M	POM&E—Elec. & Mech. Equip.
Moulds		F&B—Other Operating Expenses
Mouse Traps	Rooms—Operating Supplies	Rooms; F&B—Operating Supplies
Mucilage	General—Prtg., Stat. & Post.	Rooms; F&B—Operating Supplies; A&G—Prtg. & Stat.
Muddlers		F&B—Other Operating Expenses
Municipal Licenses— Beverages		F&B—Licenses
Municipal Taxes—Beverages		F&B—Licenses
Music & Entertainment		F&B—Music & Entertainment
Music Licenses		F&B—Music & Entertainment
Music—Mechanical	Rooms—Misc.	F&B—Music & Entertainment
Music—Sheet		F&B—Music & Entertainment
Musicians		F&B—Music & Entertainment

N

Items	No Restaurant Operation	Restaurant Operation
Napkins—Linen		F&B—China, Glass, Silver & Linen
Napkins—Paper		F&B—Operating Supplies
Napkins—Paper (Cocktail) ..		F&B—Operating Supplies
Napkins—Sanitary (Vending Machines)	Other Income	Rentals & Other Income— Vending Machines
Needles—Brochette		F&B—Other Operating Expenses

Items	No Restaurant Operation	Restaurant Operation
Needles—Linen Room	Rooms—Misc.	Rooms—Other Operating Expenses
Needles & Thread	POM&E—R&M	POM&E—Furniture, Fixtures, Equip. & Decor
Needles & Thread (Guest)	Rooms—Operating Supplies	Rooms—Operating Supplies
Newspaper Advertising	General—Mktg.	Mktg.—Adv.—Print
Newspapers for Clippings	General—Mktg.	Mktg.—Sales—Other Selling Expenses; Adv.—Other Adv. Expense; etc.
Newspapers (Guest)	Rooms—Operating Supplies	Rooms; F&B—Operating Supplies
Newspapers (for Resale)	Cost of Other Mdse. Purchased For Resale	Rentals & Other Income
Night Apparel	Rooms—Operating Supplies	Rooms—Operating Suppies
Night Auditors' Reports	General—Prtg., Stat. & Post.	A&G—Prtg. & Stat.
Noise Makers		F&B—Operating Supplies
Notary Fees	General—Professional Fees	A&G—Professional Fees
Notary Fees—Collection of Accounts	General—Misc.	A&G—Misc.
Note Interest	Fixed Charges—Interest	Interest Expense—Notes Payable
Notices (Advertising)	General—Mktg.	Mktg.—Adv.—Other Adv. Expenses
Novelties (Advertising)	General—Mktg.	Mktg.—Adv.—Other Adv. Expenses

O

Items	No Restaurant Operation	Restaurant Operation
Office Equipment Repairs	POM&E—R&M	POM&E—Elec. & Mech. Equip.
Office Glue	General—Prtg., Stat. & Post.	Rooms; F&B; etc.—Operating Supplies; A&G—Prtg. & Stat.
Office Supplies	General—Prtg., Stat. & Post.	Rooms; F&B; etc.—Operating Supplies; A&G—Prtg. & Stat.
Oil Cylinders	POM&E—Operating Supplies & Misc.	POM&E—Engineering Supplies
Oil—Fuel	POM&E—Fuel	POM&E—Fuel
Oil—Penetrating	POM&E—Operating Supplies & Misc.	POM&E—Engineering Supplies
Oil—for Resale	Cost of Gas, Oil, Auto Supplies Purchased	Gas Station—Cost of Sales
Oils & Greases—Lubrication	POM&E—Operating Supplies & Misc.	POM&E—Engineering Supplies
Oils & Greases—Lubrication (Motel Vehicles)	General—Traveling Expenses	Garage—Parking Lot—Operating Supplies
Oils—Painting & Decorating	POM&E—R&M	POM&E—Furniture, Fixtures, Equip. & Decor
Openers—Bottle		F&B—Other Operating Expenses
Openers—Bottle (Guest)	Rooms—Operating Supplies	Rooms—Operating Supplies
Openers—Can		F&B—Other Operating Expenses
Operation of Incinerators	POM&E—Operating Supplies & Misc.	POM&E—Removal of Waste Matter
Organization Expenses	Fixed Charges—Amort.	Depr. & Amort.—Amort.—Other
Outdoor Advertising	General—Mktg.	Mktg.—Adv.—Outdoor
Overages & Shortages—Cash	General—Misc.	A&G—Misc.
Overalls	Rooms—Uniforms	Rooms; F&B; etc.—Uniforms

Items	No Restaurant Operation	Restaurant Operation
Oxalic Acid		House Laundry—Laundry Supplies
Oyster Knives		F&B—Other Operating Expenses

P

Items	No Restaurant Operation	Restaurant Operation
Packing	POM&E—Operating Supplies & Misc.	POM&E—Engineering Supplies
Packing Supplies		Gift Shop—Operating Supplies
Pails	Rooms—Operating Supplies .	Rooms; F&B—Operating Supplies
Pails—Painting & Decorating	POM&E—R&M	POM&E—Furniture, Fixtures, Equip. & Decor
Paint	POM&E—R&M	POM&E—Furniture, Fixtures, Equip. & Decor
Paint Brushes	POM&E—R&M	POM&E—Furniture, Fixtures, Equip. & Decor
Paint Cleaner	Rooms—Operating Supplies .	Rooms; F&B—Operating Supplies
Painting & Decorating	POM&E—R&M	POM&E—Furniture, Fixtures, Equip. & Decor
Painting—Canvas	POM&E—R&M	POM&E—Furniture, Fixtures, Equip. & Decor
Painting & Decorating—Oils	POM&E—R&M	POM&E—Furniture, Fixtures, Equip. & Decor
Pajamas (Guest)	Rooms—Operating Supplies .	Rooms—Operating Supplies
Palms	Rooms—Misc.	Rooms; F&B; etc.—Other Operating Expenses
Pamphlets	General—Mktg.	Mktg.—Merchandising
Pamphlets—Educational or Instruction (for Employees)	Employee Benefits	Employee Benefits—Misc.
Pans		F&B—Other Operating Expenses
Pants	Rooms—Uniforms	Rooms; F&B; etc.—Uniforms
Paper Bags		F&B—Operating Supplies
Paper Butter Chips		F&B—Operating Supplies
Paper Cases		F&B—Operating Supplies
Paper Clips	General—Prtg., Stat. & Post.	Rooms; F&B; etc.—Operating Supplies; A&G—Prtg. & Stat.
Paper—Cooking		F&B—Operating Supplies
Paper Cups		Gift Shop; F&B—Operating Supplies
Paper Cups (Employees)	Rooms; General—Misc.	Rooms; F&B; etc.—Other Operating Expenses
Paper Cups (Guest)	Rooms—Operating Supplies .	Rooms; F&B—Operating Supplies
Paper Doilies		F&B—Operating Supplies
Paper Liners		F&B—Operating Supplies
Paper Napkins		F&B—Operating Supplies
Paper Napkins—Cocktail ...		F&B—Operating Supplies
Paper Plates		F&B—Operating Supplies
Paper—Shelf	Rooms—Operating Supplies .	Rooms—Operating Suppies
Paper & Straw Fans (Guest)	Rooms—Operating Supplies .	Rooms—Operating Supplies
Paper Supplies	Rooms—Operating Supplies .	Rooms; F&B; etc.—Operating Supplies
Paper Supplies—Food	Cost of Food Purchased & Incidental Expenses ...	F&B—Operating Supplies
Paper Towels (Employees) ..	General—Misc.	A&G—Misc.; Rooms; F&B; etc.—Other Operating Expenses

Items	No Restaurant Operation	Restaurant Operation
Paper Towels (Guest)	Rooms—Operating Supplies	Rooms; F&B; etc.—Operating Supplies
Parchment		F&B—Operating Supplies
Paste	General—Prtg., Stat. & Post.	Rooms; F&B; etc.—Operating Supplies; A&G—Prtg. & Stat.
Paste—Floor Covering Repair	POM&E—R&M	POM&E—Furniture, Fixtures, Equip. & Decor
Pastry Bags (Paper)		F&B—Operating Supplies
Pastry Boxes		F&B—Cost of Food Consumed
Pastry Tubes		F&B—Other Operating Expenses
Pen Holders (Employee)	General—Prtg., Stat. & Post.	Rooms; F&B; etc.—Operating Supplies; A&G—Prtg. & Stat.
Pen Holders (Guest)	Rooms—Operating Supplies	Rooms—Operating Supplies
Pen Points (Employee)	General—Prtg., Stat. & Post.	Rooms; F&B; etc.—Operating Supplies; A&G—Prtg. & Stat.
Pencil Sharpeners	General—Prtg., Stat. & Post.	Rooms; F&B; etc.—Operating Supplies; A&G—Prtg. & Stat.
Pencils	General—Prtg., Stat. & Post.	Rooms; F&B; etc.—Operating Supplies; A&G—Prtg. & Stat.
Pens (Employee)	General—Prtg. Stat. & Post.	Rooms; F&B; etc.—Operating Supplies; A&G—Prtg. & Stat.
Pens (Guest)	Rooms—Operating Supplies	Rooms—Operating Supplies
Pensions (Non-Union)	Employee Benefits	Employee Benefits—Non-Union Pension
Pensions (Union)	Employee Benefits	Employee Benefits—Union Pension
Periodicals—for Sale	Cost of Other Mdse. Purchased for Resale	Rentals & Other Income
Permits	Rooms—Misc.	Rooms; F&B—Other Operating Expenses
Personal Prop. Taxes	Fixed Charges—Personal Prop. Taxes	Rent, Property Taxes, etc.—Prop. Taxes—Personal Prop. Taxes
Petit Marmite Dishes		F&B—China, Glass, Silver & Linen
Phonograph Records—Lobby	Rooms—Misc.	Rooms—Other Operating Expenses
Phonograph Records—Restaurants		F&B—Music & Entertainment
Photo-Engraving	General—Mktg.	Mktg.—Adv.—Other Adv. Expenses
Photographs	General—Mktg.	Mktg.—Public Relations & Publicity
Physicians' Fees (Employees)	Employee Benefits	Employee Benefits—Misc.
Piano Rentals—Banquet		F&B—Other Operating Expenses
Non-Banquet	Rooms—Misc.	Rooms—Other Operating Expenses
Piano Rentals—Dining Rooms		F&B—Music & Entertainment
Piano Rentals—Entertainment		F&B—Music & Entertainment
Piano Tuning—Apartment	Rooms—Misc.	Rooms—Other Operating Expenses

Items	No Restaurant Operation	Restaurant Operation
Piano Tuning—Banquet		F&B—Other Operating Expenses
Piano Tuning—Non-Banquet	Rooms—Misc.	Rooms—Other Operating Expenses
Piano Tuning—Dining Rooms		F&B—Music & Entertainment
Piano Tuning—Entertainment		F&B—Music & Entertainment
Picture Frames	POM&E—R&M	POM&E—Furniture, Fixtures, Equip. & Decor
Pillow Cases	Rooms—China, Glassware & Linen	Rooms—China, Glassware & Linen
Pin Cushions	Rooms—Misc.	Rooms—Other Operating Expenses
Pins (Employee)	General—Prtg., Stat. & Post.	F&B; Rooms; etc.—Operating Supplies; A&G—Prtg. & Stat.
Pins (Guest)	Rooms—Operating Supplies	Rooms—Operating Supplies
Pins—Laundry		House Laundry—Laundry Supplies
Pipe Repairs	POM&E—R&M	POM&E—Elec. & Mech. Equip.
Pitchers	Rooms—China, Glassware & Linen	Rooms—China, Glassware & Linen; F&B—China, Glass, Silver & Linen
Placards	General—Mktg.	Mktg.—Merchandising
Place Cards	Rooms—Operating Supplies	Rooms—Operating Supplies
Place Cards—Bridge (Guest)	Rooms—Operating Supplies	Room; F&B—Operating Supplies
Plans—Floor	Rooms—Operating Supplies	Rooms—Operating Supplies
Plans—House (for Outside Mailing)	General—Mktg.	Mktg.—Merchandising
Plantings	POM&E—R&M	POM&E—Grounds & Landscaping
Plants	Rooms—Misc.	Rooms; F&B; etc.—Other Operating Expenses
Plaster Repairs	POM&E—R&M	POM&E—Building
Plates		F&B—China, Glass, Silver & Linen
Plates—Paper		F&B—Operating Supplies
Platters		F&B—China, Glass, Silver & Linen
Playgrounds—Maintenance	POM&E—R&M	POM&E—Grounds & Landscaping
Playing Cards	Rooms—Operating Supplies	Rooms; F&B—Operating Supplies
Plumbing Repairs	POM&E—R&M	POM&E—Elec. & Mech. Equip.
Pneumatic Tube Carriers	General—Misc.	A&G—Misc.
Pneumatic Tube Repairs	POM&E—R&M	POM&E—Elec. & Mech. Equip.
Pneumatic Tube Service	General—Misc.	A&G—Misc.
Postal Cards	General—Mktg.	Mktg.—Merchandising
Poker Chips	Rooms—Operating Supplies	Rooms—Operating Supplies
Poles—Curtains	POM&E—R&M	POM&E—Furniture, Fixtures, Equip. & Decor
Polish—Brass	Rooms—Operating Supplies	Rooms; F&B—Operating Supplies
Polish—Floor	Rooms—Operating Supplies	Rooms; F&B—Operating Supplies

Items	No Restaurant Operation	Restaurant Operation
Polish—Furniture	Rooms—Operating Supplies	Rooms; F&B—Operating Supplies
Polish—Metal	Rooms—Operating Supplies	Rooms; F&B—Operating Supplies
Portieres	POM&E—R&M	POM&E—Furniture, Fixtures, Equip. & Decor
Post Office Box Rental	General—Misc.	A&G—Misc.
Postage	General—Prtg., Stat. & Post.	A&G—Postage & Telegrams
Postage Due for Guest Mail	Rooms—Misc.	Rooms—Other Operating Expenses
Postage Meter Rentals	General—Prtg., Stat. & Post.	A&G—Postage & Telegrams
Postage—for Promotional Mailings	General—Mktg.	Mktg.—Other Selling & Promotion Expenses
Postcards (Guests)	Rooms—Operating Supplies	Rooms—Operating Supplies
Postcards—for Resale	Cost of Other Mdse. Purchased for Resale	Rentals & Other Income
Posters—Safety	General—Misc.	A&G—Misc.
Pots		F&B—Other Operating Expenses
Pouches—Key	Rooms—Uniforms	Rooms; F&B—Uniforms
Powder—Talcum (Guest)	Rooms—Operating Supplies	Rooms—Operating Supplies
Power, Cost of	POM&E—Electricity	POM&E—Electric Current
Preopening Expenses	Fixed Charges—Amort.	Depr. & Amort.—Amort.—Preopening Expenses
Preparation of Copy	General—Mktg.	Mktg.—Adv.—Other Adv. Expenses
Pressing Machine Covers	Rooms—Laundry & Dry Cleaning	House Laundry—Laundry Supplies
Printed Forms	Rooms—Operating Supplies; General—Prtg. Stat. & Post.	Rooms; F&B; etc.—Operating Supplies; A&G—Prtg. & Stat.
Printed Matter—Advertising	General—Mktg.	Mktg.—Adv.—Other Adv. Expenses
Printing & Stationery	Rooms—Misc.; General—Prtg., Stat. & Post.	Rooms; F&B; etc.—Operating Supplies; A&G—Prtg. & Stat.
Prizes—Bridge (Guest)	Rooms—Operating Supplies	Rooms; F&B—Operating Supplies
Prizes—Employee Awards for Suggestions	Employee Benefits	Employee Benefits—Misc.
Professional Entertainers		F&B—Music & Entertainment
Programs—Entertainment	General—Misc.	F&B—Music & Entertainment
Protective Service	General—Misc.	A&G—Misc.
Protectors—Mattresses	Rooms—China, Glassware & Linen	Rooms—China, Glassware & Linen
Protectors—Table		F&B—China, Glass, Silver & Linen
Protest Fees	General—Misc.	A&G—Misc.
Provision for Doubtful Accounts	General—Misc.	A&G—Provision for Doubtful Accounts
Public Address System Repairs	POM&E—R&M	POM&E—Elec. & Mech. Equip.
Public Liability Insurance	General—Insurance—General	A&G—Insurance—General
Public Rooms Cleaning (on Contract)— Banquet		F&B—Contract Cleaning
Non-Banquet	Rooms—Contract Cleaning	Rooms—Contract Cleaning

Items	*No Restaurant Operation*	*Restaurant Operation*
Public Rooms Expenses—		
Banquet		F&B—Other Operating Expenses
Non-Banquet	Rooms—Misc.	Rooms—Other Operating Expenses
Public Room Licenses		
Banquet		F&B—Licenses
Non-Banquet	Rooms—Misc.	Rooms—Other Operating Expenses
Publications—House (for Employees)	Employee Benefits	Employee Benefits—Misc.
Publications—House (for Guest Distribution)	General—Mktg.	Mktg.—Merchandising
Pump Repairs	POM&E—R&M	POM&E—Elec. & Mech. Equip.
Purifiers & Softeners for Water	POM&E—Operating Supplies; Misc.— Swimming Pool Expense ..	POM&E—Engineering Supplies

R

Items	*No Restaurant Operation*	*Restaurant Operation*
Rack Cards	Rooms—Operating Supplies .	Rooms—Operating Supplies
Rack Slips	Rooms—Operating Supplies .	Rooms—Operating Supplies
Radio Broadcasting	General—Mktg.	Mktg.—Adv.—Radio & TV
Radio Reception Expense ...	Rooms—Misc.	Rooms—Other Operating Expense; F&B—Music & Entertainment
Radio Repairs	POM&E—R&M	POM&E—Elec. & Mech. Equip.
Radiograms	General—Prtg., Stat. & Post.	A&G—Postage & Telegrams
Rags—Cleaning	Rooms—Operating Supplies .	Rooms; F&B—Operating Supplies
Rags—Shaving	Rooms—Operating Supplies .	Rooms—Operating Supplies
Railroad Train Advertising ..	General—Mktg.	Mktg.—Adv.—Outdoor
Raincoats	Rooms—Uniforms	Rooms—Uniforms
Ramekins		F&B—Operating Supplies
Range Repairs		POM&E—Elec. & Mech. Equip.
Razor Blades (Guest)	Rooms—Operating Supplies .	Rooms—Operating Supplies
Real Estate Rent (Land & Motel Buildings)	Fixed Charges—Rent	Rent, Prop. Taxes, etc.—Rent— Real Estate
Real Estate Taxes	Fixed Charges — Real Estate Taxes	Rent. Prop. Taxes, etc.—Prop. Taxes—Real Estate Taxes
Record Books	Rooms—Operating Supplies; Gen.—Prtg., Stat. & Post.	Rooms; F&B; etc.—Operating Supplies; A&G—Prtg. & Stat.
Records		F&B—Music & Entertainment
Refrigerants	POM&E—Operating Supplies & Misc.	POM&E—Misc.
Refrigeration—Electricity (Kitchenette Apts.)	Rooms—Misc.	Rooms—Other Operating Expenses
Refrigeration—Gas (Kitchenette Apts.)	Rooms—Misc.	Rooms—Other Operating Expenses
Refrigeration Supplies	POM&E—Operating Supplies & Misc.	POM&E—Operating Supplies
Refuse Removal	POM&E—Operating Supplies & Misc.	POM&E—Removal of Waste Matter

Items	No Restaurant Operation	Restaurant Operation
Register—Guest	Rooms—Misc.	Rooms—Operating Supplies
Register Maintenance Cash & Checking	POM&E—R&M	POM&E—Elec. & Mech. Equip.
Register Repairs — Cash & Checking	POM&E—R&M	POM&E—Elec. & Mech. Equip.
Registered Cable Address ...	General—Misc.	A&G—Misc.
Registrar's Fees & Expenses	General—Misc.	A&G—Misc.
Registration Cards	Rooms—Operating Supplies .	Rooms—Operating Supplies
Removal of Ashes	POM&E—Operating Supplies & Misc.	POM&E—Removal of Waste Matter
Removal of Garbage	POM&E—Operating Supplies & Misc.	POM&E—Removal of Waste Matter
Removal of Rubbish	POM&E—Operating Supplies & Misc.	POM&E—Removal of Waste Matter
Removal of Waste Matter ...	POM&E—Operating Supplies & Misc.	POM&E—Removal of Waste Matter
Rent—Building & Land	Fixed Charges—Rent	Rent, Prop. Taxes, etc.— Rent—Real Estate
Rent—Computer Equipment	Fixed Charges—Rent	Rent, Prop. Taxes, etc.— Rent—EDP Equip.
Rentals—Automatic Telephones	General—Misc.	A&G—Misc.
Rentals—Bridge Tables	Rooms—Misc.	Rooms; F&B—Other Operating Expenses
Rentals—Dictographs	General—Misc.	A&G—Misc.
Rentals—Furniture for Public Rooms (Banquet)		Rooms; F&B—Other Operating Expenses
(Non-Banquet)	Rooms—Misc.	Rooms; F&B—Other Operating Expenses
Rentals—Gas Ranges		F&B—Other Operating Expenses
Rentals—Gas Ranges (In Kitchenette Apts.)	Rooms—Misc.	Rooms—Other Operating Expenses
Rentals—Mail Chute	General—Misc.	A&G—Misc.
Rentals—Meters	POM&E—Operating Supplies & Misc.	POM&E—Misc.
Rentals—Pianos (Dining Rooms)		F&B—Music & Entertainment
Rentals—Pianos (Public Rooms)	Rooms—Misc.	Rooms; F&B—Other Operating Expenses
Rentals—Spotlights	Rooms—Misc.	Rooms; F&B—Misc.
Rentals—Teletype	General—Misc.	F&B—Banquet Expense A&G—Misc.
Rental—Telephone Equip. Charges	General—Telephone & Telegrams	Telephone—Rental of Equip.
Replacement of Window Glass	POM&E—R&M	POM&E—Building
Replating Silver		F&B—China, Glass, Silver & Linen
Report Covers	General—Prtg., Stat. & Post.	A&G—Prtg. & Stat.
Reports	General—Prtg., Stat. & Post.	A&G—Prtg. & Stat.

Items	No Restaurant Operation	Restaurant Operation
Reservation Cards—Dining Room Tables		F&B—Operating Supplies
Reservation Expense	Rooms—Reservation Expense	Rooms—Reservation Expense
Reservation Forms	Rooms—Operating Supplies .	Rooms—Operating Supplies
Reservation Tabs	Rooms—Operating Supplies .	Rooms—Operating Supplies
Resilvering Mirrors	POM&E—R&M	POM&E—Furniture, Fixtures, Equip. & Decor
Restaurant Checks		F&B—Operating Supplies
Restaurant Signs		F&B—Other Operating Expenses
Rests—Arm	POM&E—R&M	POM&E—Furniture, Fixtures, Equip. & Decor
Retinning—Utensils		F&B—Other Operating Expenses
Reweaving—Uniforms	Rooms—Uniforms	Rooms; F&B; etc.—Uniforms
Ribbon	Cost of Other Mdse. Purchased for Resale	Gift Shop—Cost of Goods for Resale
Ribbon—Billing Machines ..	General—Prtg., Stat. & Post.	A&G—Prtg. & Stat.
Ribbons—Typewriter, Checking & Cash Register	Rooms—Operating Supplies; Gen.—Prtg., Stat. & Post.	Rooms; F&B—Operating Supplies; A&G; etc.—Prtg. & Stat.
Rings—Window Shades Screens & Awnings	POM&E—R&M	POM&E—Furniture, Fixtures, Equip. & Decor
Rivet Glue	POM&E—R&M	POM&E—Furniture, Fixtures, Equip. & Decor
Rivets	POM&E—R&M	POM&E—Elec. & Mech. Equip.
Road Signs	General—Mktg.	Mktg.—Adv.—Outdoor
Roadways—Maintenance ...	POM&E—R&M	POM&E—Grounds & Landscaping
Rock Salt	POM&E—Operating Supplies & Misc.	POM&E—Misc.; F&B—Other Operating Expenses
Rollers	POM&E—R&M	POM&E—Furniture, Fixtures, Equip. & Decor
Rollers—Shades	POM&E—R&M	POM&E—Furniture, Fixtures, Equip. & Decor
Roof Repairs	POM&E—R&M	POM&E—Building
Room & Count Sheets	Rooms—Operating Supplies .	Rooms—Operating Supplies
Room Clerk Reports	Rooms—Operating Supplies .	Rooms—Operating Supplies
Room Service Order Blanks (Pads)		F&B—Operating Supplies
Rooms Guides	Rooms—Misc.	Rooms—Other Operating Expenses
Rope	POM&E—Operating Supplies & Misc.	POM&E—Misc.
Royalties		F&B—Music & Entertainment
Rubber Bands	General—Prtg., Stat. & Post.	Rooms; F&B—Operating Supplies; A&G—Prtg. & Stat.
Rubber Belts	POM&E—R&M	POM&E—Elec. & Mech. Equip.
Rubber Boots	Rooms—Uniforms; POM&E —Operating Supplies & Misc.	Rooms; F&B—Uniforms; POM&E—Uniforms
Rubber Coats (for Doormen)	Rooms—Uniforms	Rooms—Uniforms

Items	No Restaurant Operation	Restaurant Operation
Rubber Foam Seat Cushions	POM&E—R&M	POM&E—Furniture, Fixtures, Equip. & Decor
Rubber Gloves	POM&E—Uniforms	F&B; POM&E—Uniforms
Rubber Mats	POM&E—R&M	POM&E—Furniture, Fixtures, Equip. & Decor
Rubber Stamps	General—Prtg., Stat. & Post.; Rooms—Operating Supplies	Rooms; F&B—Operating Supplies; A&G—Prtg. & Stat.
Rubber Stoppers	Rooms—Operating Supplies	Rooms—Operating Supplies
Rubber Tiling	POM&E—R&M	POM&E—Furniture, Fixtures, Equip. & Decor
Rubbish Removal	POM&E—Operating Supplies & Misc.	POM&E—Removal of Waste Matter
Rug Repairs	POM&E—R&M	POM&E—Furniture, Fixtures, Equip. & Decor
Rulers	Rooms—Operating Supplies	Rooms; F&B—Operating Supplies; A&G—Prtg. & Stat.
Rules—Wooden Folding	POM&E—Operating Supplies & Misc.	POM&E—Operating Supplies

S

Items	No Restaurant Operation	Restaurant Operation
Safe-Deposit Box Keys	Rooms—Misc.	Rooms—Other Operating Expenses
Safe-Deposit Box Opening	POM&E—R&M	POM&E—Elec. & Mech. Equip.
Safe-Deposit Box Rentals	General—Misc.	A&G—Misc.
Safe-Deposit Box Repairs	POM&E—R&M	POM&E—Elec. & Mech. Equip.
Safety Envelopes	Rooms—Operating Supplies	Rooms—Operating Supplies
Safety Matches (Guest)	Rooms—Operating Supplies	Rooms; F&B—Operating Supplies
Salad Bowls		F&B—China, Glass, Silver & Linen
Sales Checks		F&B; Gift Shop—Operating Supplies
Sales Kits	General—Mktg.	Mktg.—Merchandising
Sales Tax	Fixed Charges—Sales Tax	Rent, Property Taxes, etc.—Property Taxes—Other
Salt (Laundry)		House Laundry—Laundry Supplies
Salt—Rock	POM&E—Operating Supplies & Misc.	F&B—Other Operating Expenses; POM&E—Misc
Sand	Rooms—Operating Supplies	Rooms; F&B—Operating Supplies
Sand	POM&E—R&M	POM&E—Building
Sand—Blasting	POM&E—R&M	POM&E—Building
Sand—Fire Buckets	General—Misc.	A&G—Misc.
Sand Jars	Rooms—Misc.	Rooms—Other Operating Expenses
Sand Soap	Rooms—Operating Supplies	Rooms; F&B—Operating Supplies
Sandpaper	POM&E—R&M	POM&E—Building; Furniture, Fixtures, Equip. & Decor
Sani-racks—Repairs		POM&E—Elec. & Mech. Equip.
Sanitary Inspections—Private		F&B—Other Operating Expenses

Items	No Restaurant Operation	Restaurant Operation
Sanitary Napkins (Guest)	Rooms—Operating Supplies .	Rooms—Operating Supplies
Sanitary Napkins—Vending Machines	Other Income—Vending Machines	Rentals & Other Income—Vending Machines
Sash-Steel	POM&E—R&M	POM&E—Building
Saucers		F&B—China, Glass, Silver & Linen
Sawdust		F&B—Other Operating Expenses
Scenery Rental—Public Rooms Banquet		F&B—Other Operating Expenses
Non-Banquet	Rooms—Misc.	Rooms—Other Operating Expenses
Scissors	Rooms; etc.—Misc.	Rooms; F&B; etc.—Other Operating Expenses
Score Pads	Rooms—Operating Supplies .	Rooms; F&B—Operating Supplies
Scotch Tape	General—Prtg., Stat. & Post.	Gift Shop—Operating Supplies; A&G—Prtg. & Stat.
Scrapers—Beer Foam		F&B—Other Operating Expenses
Scrapers—Paint	POM&E—R&M	POM&E—Furniture, Fixtures, Equip. & Decor
Scraping Floors	POM&E—R&M	POM&E—Building
Screening	POM&E—Operating Expenses & Misc.	POM&E—Misc.
Sealing Letters	General—Mktg.	Mktg.—Other Selling & Promotion Expenses
Seating Lists		F&B—Other Operating Expenses
Security—Contracted	General—Security	A&G—Security
Septic Tank Repairs	POM&E—R&M	POM&E—Removal of Waste Matter
Service Manuals (Employee)	Employee Benefits	Employee Benefits—Misc.
Sewer System Repairs	POM&E—R&M	POM&E—Removal of Waste Matter
Sewing Machine Repairs	POM&E—R&M	POM&E—Elec. & Mech. Equip.
Shades	POM&E—Operating Supplies & Misc.	POM&E—Misc.
Shakers—Beverage		F&B—Other Operating Expenses
Sharpeners—Pencil	Rooms—Misc.; General—Prtg., Stat. & Post.	Rooms; F&B; etc.—Operating Supplies; A&G—House Laundry—Prtg. & Stat.
Sharpening Knives		F&B—Other Operating Expenses
Sheet Music		F&B—Music & Entertainment
Sheets—Linen	Rooms—China, Glassware & Linen	Rooms—China, Glassware & Linen
Shelf Paper	Rooms—Operating Supplies .	Rooms—Operating Supplies
Shipping Tags—String Loops	Rooms—Misc.	Rooms—Other Operating Expenses
Shirt Bands		House Laundry—Laundry Supplies
Shirt Fronts	Rooms—Uniforms	Rooms; F&B—Uniforms
Shirt Fronts—Laundry		House Laundry—Laundry Supplies

Items	*No Restaurant Operation*	*Restaurant Operation*
Shoe Cloths (Guest)	Rooms—Operating Supplies .	Rooms—Operating Supplies
Shoes	Rooms—Uniforms	Rooms; F&B—Uniforms
Shortages & Overages—Cash	General—Misc.	A&G—Misc.
Shot (BB)		F&B—Operating Supplies
Shovels	POM&E—Operating Supplies & Misc.	POM&E—Engineering Supplies
Shower Curtains	Rooms—China, Glassware & Linen	Rooms—China, Glassware & Linen
Shrubbery	POM&E—R&M	POM&E—Grounds & Landscaping
Sidewalk Repairs	POM&E—R&M	POM&E—Building
Sign Repairs	POM&E—R&M	POM&E—Elec. & Mech. Equip.
Signature Books		F&B—Operating Supplies
Signing Letters	General—Mktg.	Mktg.—Other Selling & Promotion Expenses
Signs—Beverages		F&B—Other Operating Expenses
Signs—Directional (in Motel)	General—Mktg.	Mktg.—Merchandising
Signs—Restaurant		F&B—Other Operating Expenses
Signs—Road (Off Premises) .	General—Mktg.	Mktg.—Merchandising
Signs—Road (On Premises) ..	General—Mktg.	Mktg.—Merchandising
Silver Cleaners		F&B—Operating Supplies
Silver Dishes		F&B—China, Glass, Silver & Linen
Silver Forks		F&B—China, Glass, Silver & Linen
Silver Knives		F&B—China, Glass, Silver & Linen
Silver Ladles		F&B—China, Glass, Silver & Linen
Silver Plating		F&B—China, Glass, Silver & Linen
Silver Platters		F&B—China, Glass, Silver & Linen
Silver Spoons		F&B—China, Glass, Silver & Linen
Silver Teapots		F&B—China, Glass, Silver & Linen
Silver Trays		F&B—China, Glass, Silver & Linen
Silverwash		F&B—Operating Supplies
Sketches	General—Mktg.	Mktg.—Adv.—Other Adv. Expenses
Skewers		F&B—Other Operating Expenses
Slippers—Shower	Rooms—Operating Supplies .	Rooms—Operating Supplies
Smocks	Rooms—Uniforms	Rooms; F&B; House Laundry —Uniforms
Smokestack Repairs	POM&E—R&M	POM&E—Building
Snippers		F&B—Operating Supplies
Snow Removal	POM&E—R&M	POM&E—Grounds & Landscaping
Soap for Cleaning	Rooms—Operating Supplies .	Rooms; F&B—Operating Supplies
Soap (Guest)	Rooms—Operating Supplies .	Rooms—Operating Supplies
Soap (Laundry)		House Laundry—Laundry Supplies
Soaps & Powders for Washing	Rooms—Operating Supplies .	Rooms; F&B—Operating Supplies

Items	*No Restaurant Operation*	*Restaurant Operation*
Social & Sports Activities — Employees	Employee Benefits	Employee Benefits—Misc.
Soda Fountain Repairs		POM&E—Elec. & Mech. Equip.
Soda—Laundry		House Laundry—Laundry Supplies
Soda—Washing	Rooms—Operating Supplies	Rooms; F&B—Operating Supplies
Soft Drinks—Food	Cost of Food Purchased & Incidental Expenses	F&B—Cost of Mdse. Consumed
Solvents	POM&E—Operating Supplies & Misc.	POM&E—Engineering Supplies
Songbirds	Rooms—Misc.	Rooms; F&B—Other Operating Expenses
Souffle Cases		F&B—Operating Supplies
Souvenirs	Rooms—Operating Supplies	Rooms; F&B—Operating Supplies
Souvenirs (Advertising)	General—Mktg.	Mktg.—Merchandising
Special Detective Service	General—Misc.	A&G—Misc.
Special Officers—Service	Rooms—Misc.	Rooms—Other Operating Expenses
Sponges—Cleaning	Rooms—Operating Supplies	Rooms; F&B—Operating Supplies
Sponges—Painters	POM&E—R&M	POM&E—Furniture, Fixtures, Equip. & Decor
Spoons—Beverage		F&B—Other Operating Expenses
Spoons—Kitchen		F&B—Other Operating Expenses
Spoons—Mixing		F&B—Other Operating Expenses
Spoons—Silver		F&B—China, Glass, Silver & Linen
Sports Activities & Equipment—Employees	Employee Benefits	Employee Benefits—Misc.
Spotlight Rentals— Banquet		F&B—Other Operating Expenses
Non-Banquet	Rooms—Misc.	Rooms—Other Operating Expenses
Spotlights— Banquet		F&B—Other Operating Expenses
Non-Banquet	Rooms—Misc.	Rooms—Other Operating Expenses
Springs—Bed	POM&E—R&M	POM&E—Furniture, Fixtures, Equip. & Decor
Springs, Mattresses & Pillow Repairs	POM&E—R&M	POM&E—Furniture, Fixtures, Equip. & Decor
Sprinkling Street	General—Misc.	F&B—Misc.
Squeezers		F&B—Other Operating Expenses
Stairway Repairs	POM&E—R&M	POM&E—Building
Stamp Pads	General—Prtg., Stat. & Post.	Rooms; F&B—Operating Supplies; A&G—Prtg. & Stat.
Stamps—Advertising	General—Mktg.	Mktg.—Adv.—Other Adv. Expenses
Stamps—General	General—Prtg., Stat. & Post.	A&G—Postage & Telegrams

Items	No Restaurant Operation	Restaurant Operation
Staplers	Rooms—Misc.; General—Prtg., Stat. & Post.	Rooms; F&B—Operating Supplies; A&G; etc.—Prtg. & Stat.
Staples	Rooms—Misc; General—Prtg., Stat. & Post.	Rooms; F&B—Operating Supplies; A&G; etc.—Prtg. & Stat.
Starch		House Laundry—Laundry Supplies
State Income Taxes	Income Taxes	Federal & State Income Taxes —State—Current or Deferred
State Unemployment Taxes	Employee Benefits	Employee Benefits—State Unemployment
Stationery	General—Prtg., Stat. & Post.	A&G—Prtg. & Stat.; Rooms; F&B; etc.—Operating Supplies
Stationery (Guest)	Rooms—Operating Supplies	Rooms—Operating Supplies
Steak Planks		F&B—Other Operating Expenses
Steam	POM&E—Fuel	POM&E—Steam
Steam Coils	POM&E—R&M	POM&E—Elec. & Mech. Equip.
Steam—Fitting Repairs	POM&E—R&M	POM&E—Elec. & Mech. Equip.
Steam—Kitchen		F&B—Kitchen Fuel
Steel—Sash	POM&E—R&M	POM&E—Building
Steel—Structural	POM&E—R&M	POM&E—Building
Steel—Table Tops	POM&E—R&M	POM&E—Furniture, Fixtures, Equip. & Decor
Steel Wool	Rooms—Operating Supplies	Rooms; F&B—Operating Supplies
Steel Wool—Repairs	POM&E—R&M	POM&E—Furniture, Fixtures, Equip. & Decor
Stencils	Rooms—Misc.; General—Prtg., Stat. & Post.	Rooms; F&B; etc.—Operating Supplies; A&G—Prtg. & Stat.
Stick—Swizzle		F&B—Other Operating Expenses
Stirrers, Glass—Beverages		F&B—Other Operating Expenses
Stock Pots—Repairs		POM&E—Elec. & Mech. Equip.
Stock Transfer Agents; Fees	General—Misc.	A&G—Misc.
Stoppers		F&B—Other Operating Expenses
Stoppers—Tub	POM&E—R&M	POM&E—Elec. & Mech. Equip.
Storage Charges on Food & Beverages		F&B—Cost of Sales
Storage of Equipment	General—Misc.	A&G—Misc.
Storeroom Issue Reports		F&B—Operating Supplies
Storeroom Orders		F&B—Operating Supplies
Stove Lids		POM&E—Elec. & Mech. Equip.
Stove Rings		POM&E—Elec. & Mech. Equip.
Strainers—Bars		F&B—Other Operating Expenses

Items	No Restaurant Operation	Restaurant Operation
Strainers—Beverages		F&B—Other Operating Expenses
Strainers—Kitchen		F&B—Other Operating Expenses
Strainers—Wire Mesh	Rooms—Operating Supplies .	Rooms—Operating Supplies
Straws—Bar		F&B—Operating Supplies
Street Cleaning	General—Misc.	A&G—Misc.
Street Sprinkling	General—Misc.	A&G—Misc.
Stripping—Weather	POM&E—R&M	POM&E—Building
Stuffers	General—Mktg.	Mktg.—Merchandising
Subscriptions— Mercantile Agencies	General—Misc.	A&G—Misc.
Subscriptions—Trade Publications	General—Trade Assn. Dues & Trade Publications	A&G—Trade Assn. Dues & Trade Publications
Subway Advertising	General—Mktg.	Mktg.—Adv.—Outdoors
Suction Screen	POM&E—R&M	POM&E—Elec. & Mech. Equip.
Suggestion Awards— Employees	Employee Benefits	Employee Benefits—Misc.
Suits	Rooms—Uniforms	Rooms; F&B—Uniforms
Sulphur Sticks	POM&E—Operating Supplies & Misc.	POM&E—Engineering Supplies
Surveys—Special (F&B)		F&B—Other Operating Expenses
Swatters—Fly	Rooms—Operating Supplies .	Rooms; F&B—Operating Supplies
Sweepers—Carpet	Rooms—Operating Supplies .	Rooms; F&B—Operating Supplies
Swimming Pool Repairs	POM&E—R&M	POM&E—Furniture, Fixtures, Equip. & Decor
Switchboard Repairs	POM&E—R&M	POM&E—Elec. & Mech. Equip.
Switchplates	POM&E—R&M	POM&E—Building

T

Items	No Restaurant Operation	Restaurant Operation
Table Cloths		F&B—China, Glass, Silver & Linen
Table Covers	POM&E—R&M	POM&E—Furniture, Fixtures, Equip. & Decor
Table Covers—Public Rooms Banquet		F&B—Other Operating Expenses
Non-Banquet	Rooms—Misc.	Rooms—Other Operating Expenses
Table Linen Replacements (in Kitchenette Apts.)	Rooms—Misc.	Rooms—Other Operating Expenses
Table Pads		F&B—China, Glass, Silver & Linen
Table Protectors		F&B—China, Glass, Silver & Linen
Table Tent Cards		F&B—Operating Supplies
Table Tops		F&B—China, Glass, Silver & Linen
Table Tops—Glass	POM&E—R&M	POM&E—Furniture, Fixtures, Equip. & Decor
Table Tops—Stainless Steel .	POM&E—R&M	POM&E—Furniture, Fixtures, Equip. & Decor

Items	No Restaurant Operation	Restaurant Operation
Table Tops—Wood	POM&E—R&M	POM&E—Furniture, Fixtures, Equip. & Decor
Tableware		F&B—China, Glass, Silver & Linen
Tableware Replacements (in Kitchenette Apts.)	Rooms—Misc.	Rooms—Other Operating Expenses
Tags—Baggage	Rooms—Operating Supplies	Rooms—Operating Supplies
Tags—Laundry		House Laundry—Laundry Supplies
Tags—Manila	General—Prtg., Stat. & Post.	Rooms; F&B; etc.—Operating Supplies; A&G—Prtg. & Stat.
Talcum Powder (Guest)	Rooms—Operating Supplies	Rooms—Operating Supplies
Tank—Toilet Bulbs	POM&E—R&M	POM&E—Elec. & Mech. Equip.
Tank—Toilet Covers	POM&E—R&M	POM&E—Elec. & Mech. Equip.
Tape	POM&E—R&M	POM&E—Furniture, Fixtures, Equip. & Decor
Tape—Adhesive, Paper	General—Misc.	A&G—Prtg. & Stat.
Tape—Carpet	POM&E—R&M	POM&E—Furniture, Fixtures, Equip. & Decor
Tape—Masking	POM&E—R&M	POM&E—Furniture, Fixtures, Equip. & Decor
Tape—Mystic	General—Misc.	A&G—Misc.
Tar	POM&E—R&M	POM&E—Building
Tassels	POM&E—R&M	POM&E—Furniture, Fixtures, Equip. & Decor
Tax Stamp—Bond	Fixed Charges—Amort.	Depr. & Amort.—Amort.—Other
Taxes—Beverages—State (Not Included in Purchase Price)		F&B—Cost of Beverages Sold
Taxes—Electric Current	POM&E—Electricity	POM&E—Electric Current
Taxes—Franchise	Fixed Charges—Franchise Tax	Federal & State Taxes—State—Current
Taxes—House Calls	Telephone—Cost of Calls	Telephone—Cost of Calls
Taxes—Income	Fixed Charges—Federal Income Tax	Federal & State Taxes—Federal; State—Current or Deferred
Taxicab Advertising	General—Mktg.	Mktg.—Adv.—Outdoor
Taxicab Fares	General—Misc.	A&G—Misc.
Teapots		F&B—China, Glass, Silver & Linen
Technical Books	General—Trade Assn. Dues & Trade Publications	A&G—Trade Assn. Dues & Trade Publications
Telautograph	General—Misc.	A&G—Misc.
Telautograph Paper	General—Misc.	A&G—Misc.
Telegrams	General—Telephone & Telegrams	A&G—Post. & Telegrams
Telephone Charges	General—Telephone & Telegrams	Telephone—Cost of Sales
Telephone Directories	General—Telephone & Telegrams	Telephone—Other Expenses
Telephone Directories—Out-of-Town	General—Telephone & Telegrams	Telephone—Other Expenses
Telephone Directory Advertising	General—Mktg.	Mktg.—Adv.—Print

Items	No Restaurant Operation	Restaurant Operation
Telephone Directory Covers .	General—Telephone & Telegrams	Telephone—Other Expenses
Telephone Directory Holders	General—Telephone & Telegrams	Telephone—Other Expenses
Telephone Equipment Charges	General—Telephone & Telegrams	Telephone—Rental of Equip.
Telephone Holders	General—Telephone & Telegrams	Telephone—Other Expenses
Telephone Vouchers	General—Telephone & Telegrams	Telephone—Other Expenses
Teletype Paper	General—Misc.	A&G—Misc.
Teletype Rentals	General—Misc.	A&G—Misc.
Television Rentals	Fixed Charges—Rent	Rent, Prop. Taxes, etc.—Rent—Other Rentals
Television Repairs	POM&E—R&M	POM&E—Elec. & Mech. Equip.
Theatre Program Advertising	General—Mktg.	Mktg.—Adv.—Print.
Thread & Needle	POM&E—R&M	POM&E—Furniture, Fixtures, Equip. & Decor
Thread & Needles (Guest) ...	Rooms—Operating Supplies .	Rooms—Operating Supplies
Thread—Carpets	POM&E—R&M	POM&E—Furniture, Fixtures Equip. & Decor
Thread—Laundry		House Laundry—Laundry Supplies
Thread (for Linen)	Rooms—China, Glassware & Linen	Rooms—China, Glass & Linen
Ticker Service	General—Misc.	A&G—Misc.
Tickets (for Promotion)	General—Mktg.	Mktg.—Public Relations & Publicity
Ticking	POM&E—R&M	POM&E—Furniture, Fixtures, Equip. & Decor
Ties	Rooms—Uniforms	Rooms; F&B—Uniforms
Tiling—Rubber	POM&E—R&M	POM&E—Furniture, Fixtures, Equip. & Decor
Time Clock Repairs	POM&E—R&M	POM&E—Elec. & Mech. Equip.
Time Service	General—Misc.	A&G—Misc.
Time Sharing Services	General—Misc.	A&G—Data Processing Services
Time Stamp Repairs	POM&E—R&M	POM&E—Elec. & Mech. Equip.
Time Tables	Rooms—Misc.	Rooms—Other Operating Expenses
Toilet Requisites (Guest)	Rooms—Operating Supplies .	Rooms—Operating Supplies
Toothbrushes	Rooms—Operating Supplies .	Rooms—Operating Supplies
Toothpicks		F&B—Operating Supplies
Tortoni Cases		F&B—Operating Supplies
Tour Agency Commissions ..	Rooms—Commissions	Rooms—Commissions
Tourist Guides	General—Mktg.	Mktg.—Merchandising
Towels—Linen	Rooms—China, Glassware & Linen	Rooms—China, Glassware & Linen; F&B—China, Glass, Silver & Linen
Towels—Paper	Rooms—Misc.	Rooms; F&B—Other Operating Expenses
Towels—Paper (Guest)	Rooms—Operating Supplies .	Rooms—Operating Supplies
Toys	Rooms—Operating Supplies .	Rooms—Operating Supplies
Trade Magazines & Publications Subscriptions	General—Trade Assn. Dues & Trade Publications	A&G—Trade Assn. Dues & Trade Publications

Items	*No Restaurant Operation*	*Restaurant Operation*
Traffic Sheets	General—Telephone & Telegrams	Telephone—Other Expenses
Transcripts	General—Prtg., Stat. & Post.	A&G—Prtg. & Stat.
Transfer Fees	General—Misc.	A&G—Misc.
Transfer of Equipment Charges	General—Telephone & Telegrams	Telephone—Other Expenses
Transportation Charges on Food & Beverage		F&B—Cost of Sales
Transportation of Employees	General—Traveling Expense	Rooms; F&B; etc.—Other Operating Expenses
Travel Agent Commissions ..	Rooms—Commissions	Rooms—Commissions
Traveling Expenses	General—Traveling Expenses	A&G—Travel Expenses
Traveling Expenses Business Promotion	General—Mktg.	Mktg.—Other Selling and Promotional Expenses
Trays—Aluminum		F&B—Other Operating Expenses
Trays—China, Glass or Silver	Rooms—China, Glassware & Linen	F&B—China, Glass, Silver & Linen
Trays—Dresser	Rooms—China, Glassware & Linen	Rooms—China, Glassware & Linen
Trousers	Rooms—Uniforms	Rooms; F&B—Uniforms
Trucking (Not Otherwise Distributed as Cost of Goods Purchased)	General—Misc.	A&G—Misc.
Trustee's Expenses	General—Misc.	A&G—Misc.
Trustee's Fees (Handling Bonds Interest; Etc.)	General—Misc.	A&G—Misc.
Trustee's Fees (Management of Property)	General—Misc.	A&G—Management Fees
Tubes, Boiler	POM&E—R&M	POM&E—Elec. & Mech. Equip.
Tubes—Pastry		F&B—Other Operating Expenses
Tumblers	Rooms—China, Glassware & Linen	Rooms—China, Glassware & Linen; F&B—China, Glass, Silver & Linen
Turpentine	POM&E—R&M	POM&E—Furniture, Fixtures, Equip. & Decor
Twine	Rooms; General—Misc.	Rooms; F&B—Other Operating Expenses; Gift Shop—Operating Supplies
Twine (Laundry)		House Laundry—Laundry Supplies
Typewriter Inspection	POM&E—R&M	POM&E—Elec. & Mech. Equip.
Typewriter Repairs	POM&E—R&M	POM&E—Elec. & Mech. Equip.
Typewriter—Checking & Cash Register Ribbons	General—Prtg., Stat. & Post.; Rooms—Operating Supplies	Rooms; F&B—Operating Supplies; A&G—Prtg. & Stat.

U

Uncollectible Accounts	General—Misc.	A&G—Provision for Doubtful Accounts

148

Items	No Restaurant Operation	Restaurant Operation
Uniforms	Rooms—Uniforms; General—Misc.	A&G—Misc.; Rooms; F&B; etc.—Uniforms
Uniforms Cleaning	Rooms—Uniforms	Rooms; F&B; etc.—Uniforms
Uniforms Laundering	Rooms—Laundry & Dry Cleaning	Rooms; F&B; etc.—Laundry & Dry Cleaning
Uniforms Rental	Rooms; etc.—Uniforms	Rooms; F&B; etc.—Uniforms
Uniforms Repair	Rooms—Uniforms	Rooms; F&B—Uniforms
Union (Trade) Insurance & Pension Fund (Employer's Contribution)	Employee Benefits	Employee Benefits—Union Insurance, Pension Fund
Upholstery Supplies	POM&E—R&M	POM&E—Furniture, Fixtures, Equip. & Decor
Utensils—Bar		F&B—Other Operating Expenses
Utensils—Cooking (Kitchenette Apts.)	Rooms—Misc.	Rooms—Other Operating Expenses
Utensils—Kitchen		F&B—Other Operating Expenses
Umbrellas for Doormen	Rooms—Uniforms	Rooms—Uniforms
V		
Vacuum Cleaner Accessories	Rooms—Operating Supplies	Rooms; F&B—Operating Supplies
Vacuum Cleaner Repairs	POM&E—R&M	POM&E—Furniture, Fixtures, Equip. & Decor
Valances	POM&E—R&M	POM&E—Elec. & Mech. Equip.
Valve Repairs	POM&E—R&M	POM&E—Elec. & Mech. Equip.
Varnish	POM&E—R&M	POM&E—Furniture, Fixtures, Equip. & Decor
Vases—Fibre	Rooms—Misc.	Rooms; F&B—Other Operating Expenses
Vehicle Depreciation—Hotel Vehicles	Fixed Charges—Depr.	Depr. & Amort.—Depr.—Furnishing, Fixtures & Equip.
Vehicle Repairs—Hotel Vehicles	POM&E—R&M	POM&E—Elec. & Mech. Equip.
Venetian Blinds	POM&E—Operating Supplies & Misc.	POM&E—Furniture, Fixtures, Equip. & Decor
Vouchers	Rooms—Misc.; General—Prtg., Stat. & Post.	Rooms; F&B—Operating Supplies; A&G—Prtg. & Stat.
W		
Waiters' Books		F&B—Operating Supplies
Waiters' Checks		F&B—Operating Supplies
Waiters' Commissions		F&B—Salaries & Wages
Wall Hangings	POM&E—R&M	POM&E—Furniture, Fixtures, Equip. & Decor
Wall Paper	POM&E—R&M	POM&E—Furniture, Fixtures, Equip. & Decor
Wall Repairs	POM&E—R&M	POM&E—Building
Wall Washers	Rooms—Operating Supplies	Rooms; F&B—Operating Supplies

Items	No Restaurant Operation	Restaurant Operation
Want Ads (Help Wanted)	Rooms; General—Misc.	Rooms; F&B; etc.—Other Operating Expenses; A&G—Misc.
Warehouse Costs—Beverages		F&B—Other Operating Expenses
Wash Cloths	Rooms—Operating Supplies .	Rooms—Operating Supplies
Washing Soaps & Powders ..	Rooms—Operating Supplies .	Rooms; F&B—Operating Supplies
Waste	POM&E—Operating Supplies & Misc.	POM&E—Engineering Supplies
Water	POM&E—Water	POM&E—Water
Water—Circulating Ice	POM&E—Water	POM&E—Water
Water—Drinking	POM&E—Water	POM&E—Water
Water Glasses	Rooms—China, Glassware & Linen	Rooms—China, Glassware & Linen; F&B—China, Glass, Silver & Linen
Water Pitchers	Rooms—China, Glassware & Linen	Rooms—China, Glassware & Linen; F&B—China, Glass, Silver & Linen
Water Purifiers & Softeners .	POM&E—Operating Supplies & Misc.; Swimming Pool Expense	POM&E—Engineering Supplies
Water System Repairs	POM&E—R&M	POM&E—Elec. & Mech. Equip.
Water Tests	POM&E—Water	POM&E—Water
Water Treatment Chemicals & Additives	POM&E—Operating Supplies & Misc.	POM&E—Engineering Supplies
Waterproofing Repairs	POM&E—R&M	POM&E—Building
Wax	Rooms—Operating Supplies .	Rooms; F&B—Operating Supplies
Wax Paper		F&B—Operating Supplies
Weights—Sash	POM&E—R&M	POM&E—Building
Western Union Time Service	General—Misc.	A&G—Misc.
Wicks for Chafing Dishes		F&B—Kitchen Fuel
Window Boxes	Rooms—Misc.	Rooms; F&B—Other Operating Expenses
Window Cleaners' Belts & Equipment	Rooms—Operating Supplies .	Rooms; F&B—Operating Supplies
Window Cleaning (On Contract)	Rooms—Contract Cleaning ..	Rooms; F&B—Contract Cleaning
Window Glass Replacing (Glazing)	POM&E—R&M	POM&E—Building
Window Hangings	POM&E—R&M	POM&E—Furniture, Fixtures, Equip. & Decor
Window Repairs	POM&E—R&M	POM&E—Building
Window Shades—Cleaning ..	Rooms—Operating Supplies .	Rooms; F&B—Operating Supplies
Window Shades, Screen & Awning Repairs	POM&E—Operating Supplies & Misc.	POM&E—Furniture, Fixtures, Equip. & Decor
Wine Baskets		F&B—Other Operating Expenses
Wine Cellar Supplies		F&B—Other Operating Expenses
Wine Cellar Utensils		F&B—Other Operating Expenses

Items	No Restaurant Operation	Restaurant Operation
Wine Lists		F&B—Other Operating Expenses
Wired Music—Dining Rooms		F&B—Music & Entertainment
Wired Music—Lobby	Rooms—Misc.	Rooms—Other Operating Expenses
Wiring Repairs	POM&E—R&M	POM&E—Elec. & Mech. Equip.
Wool—for Bedding	POM&E—R&M	POM&E—Furniture, Fixtures, Equip. & Decor
Workmen's Compensation Insurance	Employee Benefits	Employee Benefits— Workmen's Compensation Ins.
Wrapping Cord	Rooms—Misc.	Rooms; F&B—Other Operating Expenses; A&G—Misc.
Wrapping Paper	Rooms—Misc.	Rooms; F&B—Other Operating Expenses
Wrapping Paper (Gift Shop) .	Cost of Other Mdse. Purchased For Resale	Gift Shop—Operating Supplies
Wrapping Paper (Laundry) ..		House Laundry—Laundry Supplies
Wringers & Mop Handles ...	Rooms—Operating Supplies .	Rooms; F&B—Operating Supplies
Writing Letters	General—Mktg.	Mktg.—Sales—Other Selling Expenses
Writing Supplies (for Guests & Writing Room)	Rooms—Operating Supplies .	Rooms—Operating Supplies